How to Test and Improve Your Wine Judging Ability

Irving H. Marcus

Updated and Edited by

Heidi Butzine

HOW TO TEST AND IMPROVE YOUR WINE JUDGING ABILITY
Third Edition (2011)

Copyright © 1974, 1984 Irving H. Marcus
Copyright © 2011 Anthony Marcus and Richard Marcus.
Portions of this book Copyright © 2011 Heidi Butzine.

Edited by Heidi Butzine

Published by Guanzi Institute Press
legal@guanzipress.com
http://www.guanzipress.com
409 N Pacific Coast Highway, Suite 777, Redondo Beach, CA 90277

ISBN-10   0982673388
ISBN-13   978-0-9826733-8-6

THIRD EDITION

Printed in the United States of America.

EDITOR'S FOREWORD

In my professional roles as a wine writer and director of the Certified Wine Expert program, my mission is to make wine training attainable—not intimidating. So I was delighted when I recently re-discovered *How to Test and Improve Your Wine Judging Ability* written by author Irving H. Marcus. After doing an extensive search to develop a required reading list for the Certified Wine Expert program, I am pleased to see this book reprinted and privileged to have served as its current editor.

First published in 1974, this book made an impression on readers as being a highly-useful and respected source for heightening one's knowledge—everyday wine buffs and those in the trade—about tasting wine and gaining insight into how the judges do it.

Even if you're not looking to become an "official" wine tasting judge, the writing of Irving H. Marcus takes readers through the steps of understanding, evaluating and discussing wine. In this book, the author thoughtfully shares knowledge gained from his own journey (as a wine magazine editor by profession) learning from and observing how judges taste and evaluate wine. He honestly reveals that he's never been a professional wine judge himself (which I think connects Marcus to his reader) and sets an aspirational tone that is carried throughout the book, which is: "If you drink wine at all . . . you are already a wine judge . . . but it doesn't necessarily mean you're a good one!" These words resonate with readers; non-beginners and new comers alike who want ". . . to learn more about wine to enjoy it at its fullest" and be as good a wine judge as they can.

Still relevant today, the book simplifies the sometimes overwhelming concept of wine tasting. Therefore, I have left the original text as it was printed over 25 years ago, updating some content via my own explanatory editor's notes, adding a glossary and other supplemental references.

I am pleased to include this book on the Certified Wine Expert required reading list—and in my personal book recommendations for fellow wine enthusiasts!

Heidi Butzine
Program Director, Certified Wine Expert

Los Angeles, California
2011

Irving H. Marcus at his desk.

FOREWORD

A quick rereading of Irving Marcus' small book, "How to test and improve your wine judging ability" some twelve years after its publication confirms my earlier impression that it is one of the best guides extant for the novice who is just beginning to learn about wines and also for the more experienced consumer who, being intrigued with the many styles and types of wines, is interested in improving his ability to discriminate among them. The late Irving Marcus, longtime editor and publisher of Wines and Vines, did not consider himself a professional judge, but he had the ability to distill the essence from complicated procedures and to write about them interestingly and succinctly. *How to test and improve your wine judging ability* is just one example of his beautiful writing. In it one is lead carefully but firmly through the complicated steps of several statistically valid wine judging procedures.

The new printing retains the structure used in the first edition: The basics, next the tasting tools and patterns, followed by sensory tests for taste components and finishing with chapters on sensory tests for total wine evaluation. Minor corrections and updating improve the book and do not in the least mar the style of the original.

The world wine scene has changed dramatically in the twelve years since the initial publication of this book—wine production in the United States has moved from predominantly dessert wines to table wines, sparkling wines have become increasingly popular, and the American consumer has been offered a bewildering array of lower-cost European wines specially designed to appeal to the beginning wine drinker. Irving Marcus' original purpose in writing this little book—to help persons enjoy their wines more by becoming better tasters—is still valid. Perhaps today, even more than a decade ago, the typical American, intrigued with the vast gamut of wine available, needs this guidance. May we all find more pleasure as we learn to be more discriminating!

A. Dinsmoor Webb
Professor Emeritus, UCD

Davis, California

June 1984

PREFACE

If you drink wine at all—and presumably you do or you would not have this volume in hand—you already are a wine judge.

It may be that you had your first taste of wine only last week or even yesterday. Nevertheless, when you put the beverage in your mouth, you had a reaction, a taste reaction. To yourself mentally or to someone else vocally you made some remark about the wine—"Ugh, it's sour!" (it probably wasn't) or "M-m-m, that's great!" or something in between. Whatever it was you thought or said, you had made a judgment—and anyone who makes a judgment about wine is, willy-nilly, a wine judge.

This doesn't necessarily mean you're a *good* wine judge, the kind of wine judge vintners are going to seek out for an opinion or the kind your friends are going to ask for advice about wine. You are a beginner, with the problems in making evaluative decisions that face most beginners in most fields.

As for you who are a non-beginner, possessing a background of years of acquaintanceship with wine, you have a running start on the newcomer, yet you may still not be as good a wine judge as you can be, as you would like to be and as you should be.

No matter which of the two above classifications you fit into, it is likely that you will want to learn more about wine in order to enjoy it to its fullest.

This little treatise is intended to help you do just that.

CONTENTS

SENSORY TESTS FOR TOTAL WINE EVALUATION

PASSING ALONG WHAT YOU'VE LEARNED

INTRODUCTION

I wish I could assure you that the following writings represent the essence of personal knowledge gained from long years as a recognized wine judge. I can't; the truth is that I've never been a member of even one official wine judging panel.

I have, however, been intimately associated in a reportorial and editorial way with the wine industry for a full three decades, during which years I have had innumerable opportunities to watch connoisseurs and professional winemakers test wines and make judgments. I have also sat in as an observer when formal judging panels were selecting award winners in competitions. And I have even on one occasion participated in a test aimed at determining who among those being tested possessed the capacities to make a good wine judge. (My try didn't count; I was doing it only as a reporter.) Perhaps most importantly, I am acquainted with a considerable number of recognized wine judges and have had the opportunity to discuss evaluation of wines with them on many occasions.

Some of what I have to say, then, is a distillation of what I have learned from the above occasions and individuals. Some of the rest is my personal reaction to wine judging as a pleasurable activity. But much of what I present here has been cribbed from the writings of recognized authorities in the field of wine judging.

Like most scribblers who steal the ideas of others, I call this "research". A good part of my research for this booklet involved, for example, the rewriting in "popular" style of parts of a monograph titled *Sensory Evaluation of Wines*. This was the work of M. A. Amerine and E. B. Roessler of the University of California's Department of Viticulture and Enology and was published by the Wine Institute for the professionals working in the laboratories and cellars of California wineries. I hereby acknowledge my debt to that monograph.

But just because I had stolen some of the ideas I am about to offer you does not mean that I didn't want these ideas to be correctly presented. To make sure of this for your sake and mine, I had the gall—a good part of the makeup of any reporter—to ask members of the University of California's Department of Viticulture and Enology, plus a number of other wine authorities whose ideas are reflected herein, to check my manuscript to see that what I had stolen from them was correctly translated.

With their okays, I can present the following with considerable assurance that the described tasting basics, judging procedures and actual tests are valid.

TASTING BASICS

Chapter 1

WHY WINES DIFFER IN TASTE

Wines differ in taste for a number of reasons. The most obvious is the fact that wines are produced from a wide range of grape varieties, with each variety contributing something of its own to the taste of the beverage.

Even when a number of wines are made from the same grape variety, however, differences in taste can occur. There are a number of causes. The first is that the soil in which a specific grape grows in one area almost certainly differs in composition from the soil of a different area where the same grape is planted. This difference is transmitted to the grape and through the grape to the wine.

Another possible cause of taste variation is climate. Assuming the same grape and very similar soil conditions, climatic differences can bring about better quality grapes for a particular season in one spot than in another—and can reverse the situation the following season.

This is still not the end. Granting the same grape variety, pretty much the same soil conditions, along with quite similar climate during the growing season, cultural practices in the vineyard (pruning, cultivating, thinning, harvesting, etc.) can vary from grower to grower and this can make measurable differences in the produced wines.

So here we have, by geometric progression, innumerable possibilities of ultimate variations in a single wine type—and this before the grape gets to the winery.

Within the winery itself, the fermentation procedures, the storage practices, the aging patterns in both cask and bottle, the timing and the method of filling normally vary in some degree from one winery to another and, not unexpectedly, these variances are reflected in the wines produced by different vintners in the same area from the same grape variety.

Later, when the wine leaves the cellar of its birth to go into trade channels, there are innumerable possibilities of variation in the care and handling of this sensitive beverage before it gets into the hands of its ultimate consumer. This can on occasion result in a situation in which bottles filled from the same cask at the same time end up with such differences that even a capable judge may find it difficult to recognize them as being the same wine.

Taking the above into account, it is no wonder that wines differ in taste. However, I don't necessarily consider this a handicap since I feel that it is the infinite variety one can find in wine that gives it much of its appeal.

Chapter 2
THE BEST WAY TO LEARN

If there's a preferred way to learn how to be a good wine judge, it's to persuade someone you know who is a good judge to let you taste along with him. (One way: invite him to dinner. Have a pre-dinner tasting of a couple of wines you're planning to serve.)

Preliminarily, your co-taster should explain, step by step, what it is you should be looking for in the particular wine you are about to taste. Then, as you go through each step, he should (1) ask your opinion, (2) give you his own reaction, explaining (3) why he reached that decision, so that (4) you can repeat the step and try to find what he does in the wine.

The important thing in such a master-pupil relationship is that, after the master describes what would earn excellent-to-poor marks in a judging step, he let you give your opinion of a particular wine *before* he gives his. This way, his conclusion doesn't color yours.

It may turn out—face the facts—that you don't have the capacities to become a top wine judge or even a reasonably good judge. Regardless, you will come out of such teacher—pupil sessions (and the greater the number of such sessions you have, the better) more capable than you previously were in recognizing and evaluating the complexities of wine, which is what wine judging is all about.

Even better, you will find that the pleasures you get from imbibing wine are enhanced by what you've learned. Since in all likelihood your main interest in wine judging is to make it possible for you to get taste satisfaction in direct relationship to the quality of a wine (it's a shame to drink a top wine without being able to give the beverage its just due) you've pretty much gained a major part of your objective.

Lacking the availability of a master-teacher—or in support of such a relationship—you can, on your own or in the company of others with like interests, better your discriminatory ability regarding wines through practice.

Will practice actually increase your ability to differentiate between wines and to judge the quality of wines? The evidence is that it will. Time and again, researchers have proved to their own satisfaction that practice, if it does not make perfect, at least makes better in regard to sensory judgments of foods and beverages. Whether this is due to increased sensitivity or to increased ability appears still to be unknown but no one seems to doubt that training improves sensory acuity.

◆ ◆ ◆

TASTING TOOLS & PATTERNS

Chapter 5

THE TASTING TOOLS
YOU HAVE TO WORK WITH

In evaluating wine, or in testing your capacity to evaluate wine, you will be using four of your five senses. Nobody has yet discovered how to apply the sense of hearing to the measure of a wine but sight, smell, taste and touch all become active tools when you try to decide just how good a wine is or how good you are as a potential judge of wine quality.

Sight, smell and taste are senses you will probably accept without question as measuring tools for wine. But touch?

Touch as it is used here, and it is a valid use, refers not only to tactile capacity—that is, recognizing the feel—of something in physical contact with sensory nerves, but also includes what is called the "common chemical sense," the reaction of the mucus membranes of the mouth, nose, eyes, etc. to certain irritants. In wine this common chemical sense comes into play as you place the wine in your mouth during the tasting sequences.

In turn, let me touch briefly on these four senses and how you will use them in judging wines.

SIGHT. Your very first contact with a wine you are about to evaluate comes through your eyes. As you look at the wine in the glass, you make your first two judgments. One concerns color, the other appearance.

There's little need to explain color here, except to note that certain types of wine are traditionally expected to have certain shades of specific colors—straw, yellow, gold, amber or red. As regards the wine's appearance, here you will be engaged in giving it a rating apart from that of color and will be concerned primarily with clarity.

What you see when you look at a wine can give you clues (positive or negative) as to what you might expect of the beverage when you subsequently subject it to smelling and tasting; what you see may even be so extreme on the negative side that you will not have to sniff or taste the wine to have learned enough about it to set it aside as lacking quality.

Keep in mind, however, that though sight provides you with your first chance to evaluate a wine, it is the *least exact* of the senses you will use in making such an evaluation.

SMELL. As a child, my older son used first to lift a proffered dish to his nose before deciding to taste it or refuse it. "But you haven't *tried* it!" his mother would say exasperatedly in the latter case. The fact was that the child *had* tried it; had tested it in his own way and had found it wanting.

While the major function of your nose is to bring air to your lungs, it also brings in with the air such things as dust, vapor and smells. The dust may make you sneeze, the vapor may make your nose run and the smells may distress or delight you.

To have a recognizable smell—to be odorous—a substance has to have three things:

1. It has to be volatile; that is, be easily vaporized;
2. It has to be of such composition that its molecules will dissolve in the aqueous—the watery—mucus that films that upper passages of the nose; and
3. It has to reach these upper areas of the nose in sufficient concentration to activate the olefactory nerve—the smelling nerve—so that it can tell the brain, "Hey! here's something!" and in this fashion let you know that you have smelled.

During normal in and out breathing, only 5% to 10% of the inhaled air gets into the upper nasal area where you do your smelling. To force more air into this passage, you have to sniff consciously and deeply. This guarantees that sufficient air comes into contact with the nasal mucus to give you a reasonable chance to evaluate the character of whatever odor the air possesses. The sense of smell, which varies widely among individuals and also varies from time to time for an individual, is both extraordinarily sensitive and extraordinarily selective. Authorities insist there are some compounds you can detect as a smell when they have only one six-thousandth—perhaps only one ten-thousandth—the strength they would have to possess for you to recognize them as tastes. Experience shows that you can "adapt" to an odor—lose temporarily the ability to recognize it—quite easily, and this can become a complicating factor when you are evaluating wines. Pauses between sniffs help mitigate this human weakness.

TASTE. When you say you have tasted a substance, chances are that you both smelled and tasted it. The nose and the tongue (the latter contains most of the taste buds in the mouth) are close friends who are continuously telling each other things. The tongue sends messages to the nose along an inside connecting tunnel and the nose responds by supporting or denying the taste suspicions the tongue may have. The tongue would be nearly lost as a tasting implement if the nose were somehow prevented from doing its part in "tasting". For proof, you need only recall how limited your tasting capacities were when your nasal passages became blocked shut by a cold.

There are four primary tastes: sweetness, sourness (acidity), bitterness[†] and saltiness, with the last having almost no part in wine tasting. The other three, however, are measured both singly and in combination.

In capacity to discriminate, your sense of taste lies in the broad spectrum between the inexactness of sight and the specificity of smell.

You become aware of tasting something when its concentration is above your particular taste "threshold" for this substance. The taste threshold of an individual for any substance is the smallest concentration required for him to react consciously to it. As noted above, this threshold is a personal thing, varying between individuals and among substances for any one individual.

You may, for example, be able to recognize acidity in lower concentrations than somebody else you know, but he may do better than you in recognizing bitterness. And you may have a low threshold (greater sensitivity) for sweetness but a comparatively high one for saltiness. In addition, your sensitivity to a specific taste compound

---

[†]*Editor's Note:* The difference between "bitter" and "sour" tastes are: bitter flavors are recognized at the back of the tongue, throat and palate and have a sharp, unpleasant disagreeable taste (e.g., coffee, unsweetened cocoa, olives); sour flavors are recognized at the sides of the tongue and the taste indicates acidity (e.g., lemon, orange, grape, melon, sour milk).

can change from time to time, depending on both physiological and psychological factors.

The importance placed on the concept of taste in regard to wine is to be seen in the broad application of this term to the entire idea of evaluating wine. A branch of the Wine and Food Society, for example, will announce a wine "tasting" and everyone will know it for a chance to evaluate a number of wines using all applicable senses.

TOUCH. When the air-borne particles we call smog come into contact with the mucus membranes on the inside of your eyelids, you are likely to get a burning sensation or to find your eyes watering. What has happened is that your eyes have reacted to the "touch" of smog. Other particles, coming in contact with the mucus membranes of the nose may cause sneezing. And certain particles contained in wine and taken into the mouth can bring about "touch" reactions equally definite to those who have learned to recognize them. They can, for example, help measure the wine's "body", one of the most difficult judgments to make.

This, however, does not end the part touch plays in "tasting" wine. The feel of carbon dioxide in the mouth is, to cite one instance, the result of a real tactile—touch—impression. And there are certain muscular reactions, technically called kinesthetic impressions, that result from contact with the extract content of a wine (i.e.: the puckeriness that comes from an excess of tannin) and that help you make up your mind about a wine.

Crossing the lines of taste and touch is the "common chemical sense." This may, in the presence of excess sulfur dioxide in a wine, bring on an attack of sneezing, or with other irritants can result in choking, watering of the eyes or a feeling of "hotness" when the alcohol content is above the expected norm.

With these four tools—sight, smell, taste and touch—at the ready, let's see to what use they are to be put.

◆ ◆ ◆

Chapter 6
WHAT TO LOOK FOR

In using sight, smell, taste and touch to evaluate wines, you will be checking for certain specifics: the color of the wine and how this color matches that which a particular wine type should possess, the general appearance of the wine, the wanted and unwanted odors, the desirable and undesirable tastes, and the composition of the wine as it affects your sense of touch. To each of these separate discoveries you will be giving pluses and minuses, and in the end you will sum up your various judgments and come to a general conclusion about the beverage you are judging.

COLOR

The White Wines. There is, of course, no such thing as a "white" wine. The so-called white wines range in color from a light straw tone to a hue which is widely called gold. The very lightest shades, perhaps reminding you visually of a watery lemonade are ordinarily to be found in such as Chablis and White (Johannisberg) Riesling. A slightly deeper shade of the same tone but definitely yellow this time, perhaps bringing to mind the color of undiluted lemon juice, would be the color you would expect to find in a good dry Sauterne, a Semillon or a Sauvignon Blanc. In terms admittedly almost empty of clear definition, this would be called a medium yellow.

A fuller yellow, with a suggestion of color depth, generally earns the name of light gold, a reasonably descriptive term. Such a color belongs to medium-sweet table wines, including Sweet Sauvignon Blanc, Sweet Semillon and Sauterne.

A still stronger hue of the same color, often called "medium gold" and aptly named, possesses a roundness and depth that is in contrast to the thinner color of the lighter white wines. You should expect to find this golden hue in the sweetest of table wines.

Occasionally, you will note a touch of green in a young white wine. Some consider this a visually desirable characteristic in the drier white wines, or at least in certain of them, but not in the sweeter wines.

You may, at times, come across some white table wines too light to warrant even the straw designation, and others perhaps too dark on the tawny or brown side to be counted as gold. The lightness may—mind you, may—be due to a touch too much of sulfur dioxide, used to hold back browning of the wine. As for any suggestion of brownness, in a white wine this is often indicative of oxidation and as a general rule can be taken to mean that the wine has either passed its peak or has spoiled.

The Red Wines. In color, the red wines range from very light pink to tones of purple.

The pink hues are, not unexpectedly, to be found in wines labeled "pink" or "rosé", though on occasion the pink color may be so slight as to make the use of one of these descriptive words a borderline case. In evaluating such a wine, you can properly call the thin color "low pink." It is not a mark of approval.

Most brands of rosés fall into what is called the "medium pink" range of color. Here you should find definiteness of hue without becoming aware of red overtones. In pink wines made from certain grapes (Grenache, for example) you should be able to see a touch of orange in the color. If the pink seems to possess a shading of brown, count this as a mark against the wine.

From the proper pink of a rosé wine, the color step into the lightest of red wines is not a big one. You'll find the orange tint disappearing. Yet, while there is a definite change to a greater depth of color, the wine does not reach a really full red tone. "Low red" is a term used for describing the color of such light red wines; and if it is not necessarily a positive designation neither is it always a negative one. Some wines, such as Pinot Noir, are quite acceptable in these light red tones, though a deeper color is generally considered preferable.

Another color step forward and the tone becomes "medium red." This term encompasses shades of red that possess what may, for lack of a better term, be described as "standard". Here the colors tend to favor the purple end of the red spectrum rather than the orange, yet are definitely not purple. It is within this indefinite reach of red (as noted previously, sight is the least exact of the senses used in judging wines) that a Burgundy, a Claret, a Cabernet or a Zinfandel usually fits.

When the color tone is very strong, possibly containing a purple tint, the wine is said to possess a "high red" color. Very young wines often have a definite purple touch. Or purple can indicate that the wine was made from, or contains a blend of, grape varieties having a natural purple tint, such as Alicanté Bouschet, Rubired, Almission, Grand Noir, Salvador and possibly Petite Sirah. (Of the listed grapes, the last is most likely to be found as a varietal wine.)[†] A number of native American grapes, like Concord, produce wines with strong and positive purple tones.

Not all wines fit into these pink-red or yellow-gold color brackets. Some, particularly in the dessert and aperitif classifications, properly have amber or brownish tints. However, as regards table wines, with which these writings are exclusively concerned, it is correct for you to conclude that, when a white table wine has an amber tone or a red wine has a brownish hue, this is quite likely the result of excessive oxidation. Whether caused by a poor cork or careless handling (display bottles left in a sunny window, for example) amber-white and brown-red in a table wine is rarely indicative of anything but a problem. A table wine with either of these hues does not rate a high mark for color, though exceptions are to be made on occasion for wines of venerable years, since browning often comes as a natural sequence of the passing decades.[‡]

APPEARANCE

In judging a wine, you may check color before appearance or appearance before color; the order is of little consequence. But appearance can and should be evaluated separately from color, for the color of a wine may be satisfactory and its appearance not, or vice versa.

[†]*Editor's Note:* Varietal refers to wine made principally from one grape (versus being named after the region it comes from), most often declared on the label. A wine that is said to be varietal means that the aromas and flavor characteristics are typical or true to the particular grape variety.

[‡]*Editor's Note:* See Appendix for *Recommended Aging for Wines*

What you look for basically in checking a wine's appearance is its clarity, its freedom from visually discernible suspended or precipitated material. When such material is present in suspension, it clouds and dulls the wine. On occasion, some of the suspended material drops to the bottom of the bottle to form a precipitate. (In very old wine most if not all of the suspended material may have precipitated, leaving the wine clear but vitiated in color.)

While a precipitate usually marks a wine as being somehow imperfect, this does not always mean the wine is undrinkable. An experienced imbiber will on occasion find a wine, decanted from its deposit, to be quite sound, even delightful. A less sophisticated drinker, who likely would condemn such a wine without bothering to taste it, could well be missing a treat.

The experienced judge faced with a cloudy wine can learn quite a bit about it just by looking at it. The reason is that a number of causes of such cloudiness leave individual footprints.

If, for example, a white wine has a silky and shimmering appearance or has cottony deposits, a cellarman would out of experience place the blame on the presence of some form of *lactobacillus*. By all odds, though, the cloudiness of a white wine (where slight changes in appearance are more readily noticeable than in red wines) is likely to take the form of a milky dullness.

While this milkiness can be brought on by a number of factors, there are clues even here that can point to a specific cause. These clues generally take the form of the kind of deposit accompanying the cloudiness. Some examples:

Where there is a granular deposit, the milkiness is likely due to yeast growth occurring after the wine was bottled. Where the precipitate is reddish brown, excess of copper (very rare in U.S. wines)[†] is probably the villain. And where the deposit is crystalline, the likely cause is the dropping out of some form of tartrate. However, establishing the *cause* of cloudiness or precipitation in a wine is not what the average non-professional wine judge is concerned with in

---

[†]*Editor's Note:* Copper occurs in many if not all soils, so there are some amounts of copper in all wines. Copper was used in the 1880s in Europe to control fungus. Copper may also be used to remove Hydrogen Sulfide (which can cause undesired smells in a wine).

grading for appearance; his main objective is to decide what mark to give the wine and how to describe what he observes.

The terms generally used for describing the appearance of a wine are as follows: *brilliant* for a wine that seems free of all suspended material; *clear* as a substitute for brilliant but also for a wine which, at worst, requires careful observation to find even a suggestion of haziness; *dull* where the haziness is readily noticeable; and *cloudy* where the suspended material is markedly heavy, and particularly when it is accompanied by a deposit.

Truly old wines with a precipitate but with color still passable rate as exceptions to this generalized terminology.

ODORS

A wine ought to have some recognizable and desirable odors and may have some recognizable but undesirable odors. Obviously, the first group of odors represents a plus for the wine, the second a minus when it comes to making a judgment about the beverage.

Recognizing an odor, in the meaning of detecting its presence, and recognizing it in the meaning of relating it to its *cause* are two different things.

Both are important in order to evaluate the wine properly.

The odor (actually a complexity of many odors) of a wine comes from three sources: the constituents of the grape or grapes from which it was made, the fermentation process and the changes produced during aging, the last two being grouped under the term, *vinification*.

The odor which comes from the grape is called the aroma; that from vinification is called bouquet.*

Among odors which you should prefer *not* to find in a wine are those of sulfur dioxide (sometimes used to prevent browning in white wines and readily recognizable as a sulfur smell), oxidation (pungency), acetic acidity (vinegariness) and hydrogen sulfide (the "rotten egg" smell).

---

*Because I have found that many people are unsure which designation represents what, I have come up with a helpful mnemonic device: As the grape comes before the wine, so the beginning letter of the word for grape odor ("a" in aroma) comes before the beginning letter of the word for vinification ("b" for bouquet).

Looking now at the positive side, let's consider those odors which should be present in a wine in order to win your approval.

First, it must be recognized that all wines have a vinous (winey) odor. It's almost silly to identify a product by means of itself, but there seems to be no other word which fits the situation. By no means, though, is this one of those throwaway words. If a wine has no specifically *recognizable* source of odor, it can be and often is described simply as being "vinous".

A number of the better table wines are produced from grape varieties that generally give the wine an aroma readily recognizable as being that of the ripe grapes themselves. However, quality wines are also produced from good grapes which do not possess an easily recognizable aroma in *fruit* form but which, in the process of fermentation, give the resultant wine an odor considered to be characteristic of the particular grape.

Among the grape varieties whose ripe fruit has a readily identifiable aroma are the entire Muscat family*, Gewürztraminer, Concord and a number of French-American crosses. Also to be included in the above classification but only on a "sometime" basis are Cabernet Sauvignon and Zinfandel.

Varieties that rarely have a distinctive aroma in the fruit even when ripe, but whose properly made wines can be readily identified through odor by the experienced taster, include the following: Sylvaner, Sauvignon Blanc, White (Johannisberg) Riesling, Chardonnay, Semillon, Gamay Beaujolais, Pinot Noir and Ruby Cabernet. Some authorities add Folle Blanche, Petite Sirah and Emerald Riesling to this list.

Grape varieties with very little recognizable aroma in either the fruit or the wine include these: Aligoté, Barbera, Chenin Blanc, French Colombard, Green Hungarian, Helena, Pinot Blanc, Red Veltliner and Refosco.

(I found some disagreement among the experts I consulted as to which grapes fit into which aroma classification. This is possibly due to differences in the individual thresholds to the aromas involved.)

---

*Including Muscat Hamburg, Muscat of Alexandria, Orange Muscat and Muscat Blanc. The Muscat line has a hard-to-miss definiteness of aroma.

For most consumers in most areas of the nation, obtaining the ripe wine grapes of the mentioned varieties (except possibly Muscat of Alexandria, widely shipped as a table grape) is almost impossible, so there is little opportunity for such persons to get to know the odors (if any) given off by these grapes or their juices. About the best you can do in such a situation is to try to learn to recognize the grape odor—the aroma—of a wine while being guided by someone of experience.[†]

Even more difficult for the non-professional wine taster is the task of learning to recognize the various odors in a wine that result from the vinification process (fermentation and aging, particularly the latter) and which together form the wine's bouquet.

Fortunately, evaluating the bouquet of a wine does not call for detailed specificity on the part of the average consumer. It is within range of a reasonable proportion of proboscises to catch something of the harmonious blending of esters which result from vinification and which form a substantial part of what is pleasurably called bouquet in wine.[‡]

As a practical matter, it is considerably easier to smell what is *wrong* in a wine than what is right. There is little problem in recognizing the smell of moldiness, for example, though it is rarely to be found. Or the smell of yeastiness, woodiness (from an overly long stay in the cask), vinegariness, etc.

In judging the bouquet of a wine, then, perhaps the negative approach should be used—if you find nothing *wrong* with the bouquet, give the wine a good mark on this par to your score card.

TASTE

Wine should possess certain desirable tastes and may possess certain undesirable ones. Among the more important of the unwanted tastes are excessive tannin, which results in a wine that

---

[†]*Editor's Note:* Some grapes used for wine-making do not possess an easily recognizable fruit aroma, such as Chardonnay, Vernaccia, and certain black grapes in South America that are blended to make brandy. See *Appendix Grape Varietals & Regional Wine Styles.*

[‡]*Editor's Note:* Created by the reaction of wine acids and alcohol, esters are aromatic molecules which give a wine its bouquet. Esters typically smell fruity.

is rough or bitter or both, discernible acetic acid and its companion ethyl acetate (the vinegar taste, which you may previously have recognized as a smell), lack of total acid, which leaves a wine flat and without vitality, and a high sulfur content, which you would likely have previously noted as a smell. (Remember the nose-tickling sharpness of a just-lighted sulfur match?)

When something is definitely wrong with the taste of a wine, you should not have any trouble detecting it, even if you have only a limited knowledge of wine; the problem will come in trying to define *what* is wrong. Here you will have to depend on your taste memory and on your growing experience.

The desirable tastes include a pleasing acidity. You should readily recognize the acid content of wine since ingestible acids have a family resemblance in their effect on tongue and mouth and you can't have gone through life without having become taste conscious of what acidic things (i.e.: grapefruit, unripe apples, etc.) taste like. If a wine lacks acid it will also lack taste vitality; if it has too much acid, it will possess a certain "bite" that you will readily recognize.

Another taste factor you will be evaluating is that of the sweetness or dryness of the wine. Table wines are not all dry; some are deliberately made semi-sweet and others sweet, though it must be recognized that these are comparative terms. A wine may properly warrant the term "dry" even though chemical tests would show it to possess some tiny measure of sweetness (which a judge of experience with a low threshold for sweetness may be able to catch on tasting). Also, some wines labeled "dry" may possess definite overtones of sweetness, having been deliberately made so in the belief that Americans like to have wines called "dry" but don't actually want them to taste that way. For some beginning imbibers (and for certain regular wine drinkers) this belief has a measure of validity.

Another component of wine you will be trying to evaluate orally is that of "body". Trying to describe to you what "body" is or how you will recognize it in a wine is a nearly impossible task. I have fallen back on a dictionary definition of the word as it applies to tasting: " . . . Consistency; substance; fullness or richness . . ." If any of these words seem to fit the feel of a wine in your mouth, you probably are tasting a wine with body. I will try to clarify this a bit further in a coming section.

The measure of flavor comes next in the tasting sequence. I suppose every liquid except pure water has a flavor, so what you are tasting for in a wine is not so much to decide if there *is* a flavor, but what kind of flavor and how weak or concentrated that flavor is.

Much of what you will find as the flavor of a wine has previously shown itself, at least teasingly, as aroma and bouquet. The flavor of the grape variety and the esters created by fermentation and aging should be more pronounced as tastes than as odors and their inter-relationships with the alcoholic content of the wine will serve to bring to your taste buds a reaction that will give you varying degrees of pleasure, which you will have to translate into pluses or minuses.

The final single specific you will be looking for is the wine's astringency. In the main, this will be a measure of the tannin content of the wine. Since the tannin comes to the wine from the grape skins, it will automatically be stronger in red wines (fermented on the grape skins) than in whites (fermented after removal from the grape skins) but there may be traces of tannin in the whites also.

Don't take the above to mean that tannin, as such, is undesirable; it is not. It is *required* in a red wine, and in fact the amount of tannin a young red wine has is one of the measures of how long it will take to mature and how long it will hold its maturity. In the reds, "big" wines always start out with pronounced tannin.

What you will be checking here, then, is whether there is a *proper* amount of tannin in the particular wine, with excess or lack being equally undesirable but with the wine's age and future promise being taken into consideration.

It is here, too, that you will be using touch and its companion common chemical sense as tasting tools. One of the things you will be looking for through touch will be the alcohol content (anything over 14% will feel "hot" or "sharp" in the mouth).[†] Another is the feel of carbon dioxide on the tongue (many table wines have slight amounts of carbon dioxide, not enough to give the wine bubbles as in sparkling wine but enough to provide a definite tactile sensation). The decision on the wine's body will also be made mainly on the basis of the touch reactions of the tongue and the walls of the mouth. And you will, in addition, be checking white wines for sulfur dioxide content, used (particularly in some European table wines) to prevent browning. While you will likely have detected sulfur dioxide beforehand as an odor, this compound definitely affects the walls of the mouth through the common chemical sense.

GENERAL QUALITY

To this point, you have been checking for individual specifics. Now you embark on evaluating the wine as a whole. What you will be looking for here is your reaction to the way the specifics blend together to produce a unified whole. I presume that in actuality what you will be doing is applying a how-much-do-I-like-it yard-stick to the beverage. If that is so, I see nothing wrong in it.

[†]*Editor's Note:* If you are looking to determine a wine's sweetness (or dryness), the alcohol level can be an indicator of this. Usually, wines having an alcohol by volume (ABV) level of 11% or less tend to be sweeter, while wines having 11% to 13.5% tend to be dry (no residual sugar). Those above 13.5% can go either way, since residual sugar is often used to balance the "hot" taste of alcohol.

gargle the wine in taking this measure of the beverage. Others "chew" the wine and still others allow it to warm up in the mouth.

It is a pattern with some experienced judges to draw air through the wine held in the mouth. This churns the wine and volatizes additional odors which are then smelled as the air is exhaled through the nose, thus giving taste an added helping hand.

Where four or more wines are being judged at a time, you should spit out the wine rather than swallow it when making the evaluations noted above. Where only two or three wines are involved, some of each may be swallowed. (In tasting any substantial number of wines, the mouth should be rinsed out with water periodically. Also, in a prolonged tasting, small pieces of bread, crackers or mild cheese can be eaten between wine samplings to remove residual tastes from the mouth.)

Once the above individual components of a wine have been judged and the separate scores put down on the sheet, you are confronted with the need for giving the wine a mark for its overall quality.

In doing this, you mentally review your previous separate judgments then retaste the wine for the total impression it leaves with you. Here it makes sense to swallow some of the wine since this allows you to judge the wine's aftertaste.

If you are confronted with more than a single type of table wine to evaluate or if you are offering a number of types for others to judge, try to establish the order of tasting from dry to sweet, white to red, low to high sugar, and low to high tannin.

Red wines are usually offered at room temperature (meaning roughly in the low 70s) while whites are as usually offered chilled, perhaps at 60° or a bit below.*

◆ ◆ ◆

---

*Some vintners believe the flavor nuances of a white wine come through much more readily when the wine is served at room temperature. Proof of this belief came as I was putting the finishing touches to this manuscript. For an altogether different reason, I had called together for a casual blind tasting four of California's better known producers of quality table wines. In the general conversation that followed the tasting of two white table wines—both of which, incidentally, were correctly identified as to type and one as to brand—the point was made that the odor and flavor came through much more readily as the cooled wine was warmed by their hands. Tasting along with the vintners as an amateur, I had to agree. So perhaps—perhaps, mind you—the traditional serving of white wine for judging at a low temperature is in error.

Chapter 9

THE SCORECARD

The record of the step-by-step scoring of a wine by professionals is kept on a formalized card or sheet on which each contributing factor is separately listed along with the points assigned it.

Over the years, a variety of scorecards have been tested, with perfection rated at anything from 10 to 100 points. One of the most practical and certainly a widely used scorecard involves a 20-point scale covering ten quality-contributing factors, with each given a numerical weight reflecting its comparative importance.[†]

COLOR. 2
APPEARANCE. 2
AROMA & BOUQUET 4
ACESCENCE 2
TOTAL ACID. 2
SUGAR. 1
BODY 1
FLAVOR 2
ASTRINGENCY 2
GENERAL QUALITY. 2

This scorecard, you will note, provides in sequence four points through use of the eyes, another four through nasal determination, ten points for aspects judged orally, and a final two points for overall impression.

[†]*Editor's Note:* The author of this book explores the 20-point UC Davis scale that is commonly used in wine competitions. However, it should be noted that there are other 100-point systems and scales used by today's popular and respected wine critics. While some critics may consider the 20-point system limiting in rating something as subjective as wine, it is still regarded as a useful analytical method for giving wine a numerical rating relative to its quality. A comparison of these wine rating systems is at the end of this book—see Appendix *Wine Rating Systems.*

Using this type of scorecard permits you to concentrate on judging one quality component at a time. Also, except for the combined aroma-bouquet step, judgment in each case is a simple matter of granting or withholding either one or two points. Where there is a single point involved, your decision is essentially a matter of a "yes" or "no". Likewise, where there are two points, the decision breaks down in a "yes" worth 2 points, a "no" worth nothing or a "maybe" worth a single point.

Don't take this to mean, however, that a wine can't earn negative points in one judging phase or another. Where a wine is really poor in one of its judging classifications, it can indeed be given a minus point or two.

It should be noted, moreover, that where a wine shows up very poorly in one of its components, this can affect the points it earns in related components. You may find, for example, that a wine which is strongly vinegary not only warrants a negative point count under "acescence" but may also by possessing this unfortunate characteristic, depress the points it might otherwise have earned under total acidity, flavor and general quality.

In the pages to follow, you will find a reproduction of an actual scorecard using the above breakdown.* Note that the numerical scores are in each case accompanied by indications of why that score was given. This is an accepted pattern in formal judgings and serves as a reminder to the judge when he later discusses the wine with his fellow panel members.

By means of this sort of scorecard, a capable judge can readily determine the quality of a particular wine. In formal judgings, the scorecard provides a numerical basis for calling a wine a gold medal winner (usually, 17 or more points) or for giving it a lesser award. It can with equal readiness be used to rank a wine in relation to others being judged with it.

---

*This particular score sheet represents the judgment of a Napa Valley vintner on five 1967 Napa Valley Gamay Beaujolais wines tasted blind as still-young wines in the Spring of 1968. The session (at which I sat in as observer) involved an eleven judge panel of Napa Valley vintners and U.C. enologists. The session was one of an annual series undertaken to determine the potentials of specific varietal wines of the area's previous vintage. Incidentally, 1967 was one of the poorer climatic years in the Napa Valley.

In your case, since you are not likely to be making judgments in a professional competition, such a scorecard helps you evaluate a particular wine for your own purposes. If this happens to be a wine you are tasting for the first time and one which you're thinking of laying down in your cellar, your scoring of it will certainly give you a clue as to whether a case or two would be a wise investment (in taste *and* money).

If the answer in the latter case is yes, I suggest you date and retain the scorecard so that, at regular intervals in the future (say every six months) you can re-test the wine and, by comparing scorecards, determine if the wine is improving and can await further development, if it is merely holding its own (meaning begin to drink it now) or if it is actually becoming less good (hurry!).

SCORE CARD

		19	05⁻	43	93	67
Appearance	2	OK 2	Clear 2	Clear 2	Slightly dull 2	clear 2
Color	2	med red 2	medium to light red 1	Dark red, Bluish 2	med.+ red 2	med. red 2
Aroma and Bouquet	4	med.+ distinct 2	distinct Varietal 3	med. aroma slight H₂S 2	pronounced varietal but slight off nose 3	vinous, clean 2
Acescence	2	light 2	light 2	light 2	light 2	light 2
Total Acid	2	medium 2	medium+ 2	slightly low 1	medium − 2	medium + 2
Sugar	1	DRY 1	Dry 1	not quite dry 1	DRY 1	DRY 1
Body	1	good 1	good 1	thin tasting 0	Full 1	Slightly thin 0
Flavor	2	med − 1	Full, Rich 2	light, alcoholic 1	off flavor or after taste 1	low but clean 1
Astringency	2	Slightly Rough 1	needs age 2	an edge of roughness 2	Harsh 1	Slightly Rough 1
General Quality	2	average 1	above ave. 2	standard 0	average 1	standard to ave. 1
TOTAL		15	18	13	16	14

17 to 20, wines must have some outstanding characteristics and no marked defect; 13 to 16, standard wines with neither outstanding character or defect; 9 to 12, wines of commercial acceptibility but with a noticeable defect; 5 to 8, wines below commercial acceptibility; 1 to 4, completely spoiled wines.

34

Chapter 10

THE SCORING PATTERN

We now get to the most difficult element in judging—how to relate what you see, smell, taste and feel to the assigned point range for each quality component.

In this effort, the following guidelines should be of help even though each of your judging decisions will necessarily reflect your own interpretations of what is meant by the terms used.

APPEARANCE: A *brilliant* wine, with lights seeming to sparkle through it, is worth the full 2 points. If it is *clear* but lacks the visual sharpness of brilliance, give it 1 point. (Some judges use the term "clear" for both above evaluations.) A *dull* or *cloudy* wine gets no point. The lines of demarcation between these classifications are not sharp; there are halfway steps in which you will have a tough job deciding just where to fit the wine but this is true of all non-objective measurements.

COLOR: Each wine type has its own desirable color range. Your concern here is to evaluate both the *hue* and the *amount* of color as these fit the acceptable range.

Regarding hue in white table wines, this may be any of a number of shades of straw, yellow or gold, with the amount being measured as low, medium or high. In red table wines, pink and red are the usual hues with some touches of purple or violet, and with the amount interpreted in the vernacular of wine judging as low, medium and dark.

In the whites, an oxidized brownish tinge wins no points for color, a wine with proper hue but weak in amount of color (or vice versa) gets 1 point while a wine fulfilling both color requirements gets the full 2 points.

In red table wines, follow the same pattern—grant 2 points to a wine which meets both the hue and amount criteria, a single point if it satisfactorily meets only one, and no points if both hue and color are wrong.

Unfortunately, there is no way one can reproduce on paper colors to match the translucent color impact of the wines themselves so your color judgments will depend on your continuing experience.

ODORS: If a wine has a varietal odor which you can relate to a grape source (here, too, the inexperienced taster is under a handicap) the aroma is described as *varietal* and warrants the full count of 4 points. If the varietal odor is there but not identifiable as to grape source, the aroma is described as distinct and the wine gets 3 points. If there is no distinguishable odor, the wine is called *vinous* and earns 2 points.

The assumption above is that some degree of bouquet resulting from the vinification of the wine is present (it practically *has* to be). If, however, this vinification odor (bouquet) is very weak and the best you can give the wine for its aroma is a questioning "maybe", the wine gets only 1 or 2 points.

A zero rating for aroma and bouquet is almost impossible unless the positive odors described above are questionable all around and are accompanied by off-odors (sulfur dioxide, hydrogen sulfide, excessive woodiness, etc.). In such cases, the score previously given is reduced by 1 or 2 points and this can in extreme cases result in a zero rating.

ACESCENCE (Volatile Acidity): Here you are mainly concerned with trying to measure the volatile acidity of the wine. Since the major volative acid in wine is acetic (the "vinegar" acid) it should be familiar to you. Vinegariness is unwanted in wine; the more there is of it, the lower the wine scores. So if a wine you are tasting possesses a blatant vinegariness, give it no points. If the vinegariness is suggestively there but so weak as to make you question its presence, the wine warrants 1 point. And if you can detect no touch of this unwanted volatile acid, the wine gets the full two points. (This is the only judging component in which a complete negative finding brings positive points.)

TOTAL ACIDITY: This is a measure of the amount of *desired* acids in the wine. A wine should possess a definite acidity but within pleasing taste range. If a wine you are judging tastes flat, this indicates an insufficiency of acid and the wine garners no points; if it tastes quite sharp on the tongue, the wine probably has an excess of acid and this too earns it no points. In between these two negative extremes, the wine may have a slight acidity, worth 1 point; an edge too much acidity, also worth 1 point; or possess a positive, pleasing but not overwhelming acidity, worth the full 2 points.

SUGAR: Most types of table wines are supposed to be dry. Others are purposely produced as semi-sweet or sweet wines. This makes it important that you learn where a wine type belongs in the dry-sweet range.* Then, when you find a touch of sweetness in a wine supposed to be dry or vice versa, you will know that the wine gets a zero in the point column. Conversely, if it *fits* the dry-sweet classification for its type, it gets the single point given this taste breakdown.

BODY: In wine judging, one of the decisions most difficult to make is how to rate a wine for its "body". Body in a wine is equally difficult to describe. Essentially, what you are evaluating here is the sense of viscosity or "solidity" (if a liquid can be said to have any solidity) in the wine. Perhaps the clue to what you should be looking for lies in the fact that body in a wine can be described as "thin", "full", or "heavy".

Body depends in good part on sugar content, non-sugar extracts and percentage of alcohol. Where, as in a very dry wine, sugar content is practically non-existent, the non-sugar extracts and alcohol take on an increasing importance in measuring body.

Red wines, because they almost automatically possess comparatively high extract content, are expected to be "full" or "high" in body. White table wines, particularly if dry, do not have to have

---

*WHITE varietal table wines that should be definitely dry include Johannesberg (White) Riesling, Sylvaner, Chardonnay, Pinot Blanc, Folle Blanche and French Colombard. Semi-sweet whites include Traminer, Gewürztraminer, Sauterne (also often sweet), Sauvignon Blanc and Semillon. Sweet whites are generally so identified on the label. Some non-varietal whites such as Chablis, Moselle and Rhine wines should be dry. In the RED varietals, practically all are supposed to be dry. Some non-varietal reds are deliberately made with a slight edge of sweetness, usually described on the label by some such adjective as "mellow."

the rounded body that the sweeter whites ought to possess; in each case the point determination will depend on your knowledge of what is proper to the type.

It's obvious that your giving or denying a wine its one point for body will depend pretty much on how you personally interpret these non-exact descriptions. I realize this is hardly helpful but I have asked a number of professional judges for a better description of body in wine and I'm sorry to say that none came up with anything more definitive.[†]

FLAVOR: Here you are in part judging orally what you had previously judged nasally as varietal aroma. At the same time, you are taking a measure of the alcohol content and trying to evaluate the wine's maturity.

The grape aroma should be at least as definite as a taste as it was as an odor; normally you can expect it to be much stronger. If the wine has this fruitiness, seems to possess proper alcohol (in table wines between 10% and 14%, evaluated by the "bite" of the alcohol on the tongue), and has no negative qualities such as being yeasty or metallic, the wine warrants a full 2 points for flavor. If, for one reason or another, the flavor is there but lacks decisiveness, a single point is all the wine gets. And if whatever flavor the wine has seems to be dominated by negative factors (coarseness, stemminess, etc.) it warrants only a zero.

ASTRINGENCY: The astringency of wine is due mainly to its tannin content. You'll recognize tannin by the rough feel of the wine on the tongue and especially by the feeling of puckeriness it gives the walls of the mouth.[*]

[†]*Editor's Note:* While the body or weight of wine in the mouth is subjective to the taster, body does have an impact on mouth feel and perception of the wine during tasting. You can assess and describe body by comparing the feeling of the wine in your mouth to that of milk: light-bodied wine = skim milk, medium-bodied wine = whole milk, full-bodied wine = heavy cream.

[*]George Cooke of the Univ. of Calif.'s Dept. of Viticulture and Enology suggests that a good way to learn what astringency in a wine feels like is to buy (from the same winery, if possible) both a very young and a well-aged red varietal and then do a comparative tasting of the two.

Red wines are (and should be) more astringent than whites. Young red wines are especially astringent and since the tannin generally becomes less pronounced with the passage of time, here's a possible clue to the maturity of the wine.

A white table wine, especially a sweet or semi-sweet wine wins the full 2 points for astringency (rather for the *lack* of it) only when you find it smooth and soft on the tongue. If there is a suggestion of coarseness, the point count drops to 1, and if this coarseness is quite definite, the wine gets no points at all.

In supposedly mature red table wines, if you decide that astringency is present as a trace that helps bring character to the wine, give it 2 points. As the astringency increases beyond this and becomes more apparent, the score drops, first to 1 point for a medium rough wine and then to zero for one definitely rough.

If you are knowingly tasting a young (year-old) red wine, heavy tannin can be a plus because it indicates that the wine may have a long period of maturity once it achieves proper age.

GENERAL QUALITY: Although you have now evaluated all of the major components that go into establishing the quality of a wine, you have done so on a one-at-a-time basis. Now, as a last measure, you have to taste the wine essentially for itself, to see how all these separate factors interact with each other to make a pleasing or displeasing whole.

You may, for example, in tasting a wine for its total acid, have found it a bit too sharp, too acidic, just as you might have found the same wine, when judging it for sweetness, to be a touch too sugary for the type. In tasting the wine as a whole, however, you may find sugar and acid in fine balance.

At this stage of your sensory evaluation of a wine, you should definitely swallow some. Only in this way can you measure the wine's aftertaste, which is certainly an important part of the overall impression you will get from the wine.[†] When the aftertaste is clean,

---

[†]*Editor's Note:* Where more than three wines are tasted (and in most professional settings), it is still advisable to spit after evaluating the wine. Even spitting (also called expectorating) the wine can leave an aftertaste that is acceptable for assessing wine. To avoid palate fatigue and to prevent impaired judgment, most judges are under certain requirements not to swallow at a wine tasting.

lacks bitterness and in essence leaves you wanting more, this is a considerable plus for the wine.

If the overall impression you get from the wine is favorable, give it the full 2 points for general quality. As the impression descends through fair to poor, the points move to 1 and zero.

◆ ◆ ◆

Chapter 11

WHAT YOU WILL NEED BESIDES WINE

MEASURING DEVICES. Because you will want to measure the additions to the wines or the wines themselves meticulously, you will require certain measuring devices. For simplicity's sake, the measuring devices specified are those you will likely find in your own kitchen.

1. *A set of measuring cups.* A cup when full holds 8 oz., a half cup 4 oz. and a quarter cup 2 oz.

2. *A set of measuring spoons.* A level tablespoon contains a half ounce, a teaspoon contains 1/6 oz., with part-spoons proportionate.

GLASSES. Tulip shaped glasses are preferred because the narrow rim tends to hold in and concentrate the odors. The 8 oz. size is the one generally used but the 6 oz. or even the 4 oz. glass will do. I do not know of any tulip shaped plastic glasses but reusable slope-walled wine glasses of plastic are likely obtainable from some local dealer. You will also need water glasses, one for each taster, and a pitcher for water.

MARKER. To mark the bottles and/or glasses for identification, you can use a grease pencil, obtainable in most stationery stores, or-and this appears to be the simpler way-you can simply stick a piece of masking tape on the base of the glass or side of the bottle and write the identifying mark on it with pen or pencil.

SCORECARDS. These are simply ruled or unruled pieces of paper on which the tasting instructions, the random numbers of the wines to be tasted and the judgments of those taking the tests can be recorded. They are *not* the itemized scorecards described in Chapter 9.

CONTROL SHEET. Actually the same or similar to the scorecard. Used to record the kind of wines being offered for tasting and the sequence in which they will be presented. Also used as a check sheet to mark the individual scorecards after the tastings are completed.

BREAD OR CRACKERS AND CHEESE. These, along with the water, are to be placed at the tasters' table for cleansing the palate between tastings. The cheese should be mild, the crackers unsalted and the bread without any strong taste of its own (unless you can obtain the so-called "French" bread, which has a touch of non-objectionable sourness).

COUNTERS. These are simply small pieces of paper or (preferably) cardboard on which the wine name, an identifying number or some other message can be written. At the proper time, these are placed in a bowl, mixed thoroughly and selected blindly in order to establish a random sequence of some sort.

SPITTOON. While non-professional tasters rarely expectorate the wines they are tasting, they will want to spit out the water they use to rinse their mouths (and they should certainly spit out wines with augmented tannin). A plastic or waxed paper container of substantial size (5 to 6 inches across the mouth) will serve this purpose. If you can, provide one such container for each judge (it can be placed on the floor at his feet) or spot one at the center of the judging table where it will be within reach of all.

WORK TABLE. A dinette or kitchen table or similar working area in or near the kitchen will do. It is on this surface that the wines will be prepared and the glasses lined up, filled and readied for serving.

ADDITIVES. For purposes of bringing about controlled variations in the wines to be judged, you will have to have on hand Sugar, Citric Acid, Tannic Acid and Distilled Vinegar. The sugar and vinegar you should find in your pantry, the citric acid and the tannic acid should be available in a nearby drug store.[†]

TRAY. A serving tray facilitates the carrying out of glasses in the required order from the work area to where the tasting is being held (most likely the dining room).

◆ ◆ ◆

[†]*Editor's Note:* Citric acid may be available at specialty food stores, health food stores or other sources online, including home brewing supply stores. Be sure that it is food grade citric acid that you are using. Tannic acid may be harder to find and it is recommended that you use brewed regular black tea (in lieu of tannic acid) to add tannin to wine in this application. Use ½ teaspoon of brewed tea per half-gallon of wine.

Chapter 12

RANDOM NUMBERS

Though testing should be done "blind"—that is, without the one doing the judging having any clue as to what wine is in what glass—the person giving the test must be certain that he is not blind as to the contents of the various glasses. The usual way to reach this double-faceted goal is through the use of random numbers for identification.

Random numbers are just that—a series of numbers selected by chance so that there is no discernible pattern to their sequence which could, consciously or subconsciously, provide the taster with a clue to the contents of the proffered glasses.

You can make up your own random numbers as you go along, though it is not as easy as it sounds since on occasion a mental bent can result in a repetitive pattern showing up in the sequences.

I suggest using the random number chart shown here, which presumably provides no such clues.

In using these random numbers, it is suggested that the sequence shown in the chart be followed exactly. It is not necessary to begin with the first listed number. For any particular test, you can start at a haphazardly selected point on the chart, continuing the sequence from there on in anyone direction (vertically, horizontally or at an angle). Since the chart offers 99 numbers with no duplications, there is plenty of room for the selection of varying sequences.

The pattern for numbering the glasses presented in the upcoming chapters calls for you to give each glass containing the same wine the same number for each judge. If, for example, the first test glass containing Wine "A" is numbered 47 for one judge, it must be numbered 47 for all judges.

There is, it has been pointed out to me, a weakness in this pattern of numbering glasses. A judge sitting around a table at which other judges are also making determinations may by accident or design note what mark someone else has given one of the numbered wines and may in this manner be influenced in his own judgment of the wine carrying that number.

One researcher, trained in handling panels for serious wine judging, suggested to me that it would be better if I proposed that each wine carry a different number for each judge. Wine "A", for example, might be numbered 47 for the first judge, 23 for the second, 95 for the third, etc.

I was at first intrigued by this suggestion but when I contemplated the extra work this would involve in keeping the records straight, I went back to the simpler numbering pattern I started with.

I nevertheless determined to include the researcher's suggestion here because it may appeal to you. If you are not bothered by what seems to me to be the complicated bookkeeping involved, the use of such multiple numbers would certainly mitigate against inadvertent disclosure by one judge to another of his measure of a wine.

Should you decide to proceed in this fashion, the chart of randomly sequenced numbers on the following page should ease your problem of not duplicating any of the numbers you assign to the wines being judged.

◆ ◆ ◆

CHART OF RANDOM NUMBERS

46	58	20	59	61	04	98	35	39
23	42	12	68	93	27	24	87	57
63	13	64	26	16	74	50	70	81
47	86	06	45	38	32	95	83	40
82	73	44	89	22	07	48	66	08
21	09	96	19	92	85	36	18	76
28	94	78	43	55	97	29	79	05
62	30	84	69	71	56	75	11	17
91	10	34	52	60	31	67	80	49
72	14	01	54	37	02	41	65	90
99	33	25	88	15	53	77	51	03

The chart above contains 99 numbers with no duplications. The numbers are randomly placed and presumably do not show any repetitive sequential patterns. Any number on the chart can become the beginning point in choosing a numerical sequence, and the selection from that point can proceed vertically, horizontally or angularly .

TASTE COMPONENT TESTS

Chapter 13

A FEW PRELIMINARY WORDS ABOUT SENSORY TESTS

Sensory tests are simply those in which the senses are used to make evaluative judgments. There are various classifications of sensory tests, of which the following four are rated as most important in wine judging.

DIFFERENCE TESTS, in which the judge is asked to establish if the wine he is evaluating is the same or different from a control, or if two wines are alike or unlike.

RANKING TESTS, in which the judge is asked to rank several samples on the basis of a single characteristic—sweetness, acidity, etc., or on overall quality.

SCORING TESTS, in which the judge is asked to rate wines against either a control sample ("as good", "better", "much better", "worse", etc.) or against an ideal ("gold medal quality", etc.) as established under accepted industry standards.

HEDONIC TESTS, in which the judge simply expresses how much he likes or dislikes a wine.

This booklet concerns itself mainly with the first three classifications listed above—measuring differences of one kind or another among presented wines, ranking a number of wines on the basis of a specific characteristic, or scoring a number of wines according to their overall qualities.

All tests that follow are presented with an explanatory paragraph at the start giving the general idea of each. This may suffice as a guide for you to go ahead on your own, plotting the sequence of moves to fit your special needs and/or facilities. Otherwise, the particularized (perhaps over-particularized) steps can be followed.

Regardless of the pattern decided on, one point should be followed without exception—instructions should be given orally by whoever is conducting the test before judging begins.* This despite the fact that complete instructions are to be typed at the top of each of the judges' scorecards or sheets.

Good lighting is a must for wine judging, especially where color is one of the bases on which judgment is to be made. Each testing station should be arranged so that individuals do not interfere with one another. No talking should be permitted while the test is going on. And no smoking.

When results of tests are made known to the participants, open discussion should be encouraged.

Because olefactory and taste acuity generally decrease after a meal, it is advantageous to conduct judgings before the serving of food.

General needs for each of the tests include the following:

- Tulip shaped glasses for tasting.
- Grease pencil or masking tape and pen for numbering glasses and bottles.
- Control Sheet.
- Scorecards.
- White table cloth, particularly where color detection is part of test.
- Mild cheese, bread or crackers, water and containers for expectorating.
- A serving tray.

The tests are offered in two groupings. The first concerns itself mainly with measuring the ability of the judge to pick out differences in one of the major components of wine—acidity, sweetness, etc.—among wines presented for tasting. The second group is aimed at measuring the capability of the judge in evaluating the wines themselves.

---

*The assumption is made here that you will be readying the tests for others to take. If you are to participate as a judge yourself, someone else should do the indicated preparatory work.

For purposes of disguising wines to be identified or evaluated, judges are never shown bottles until after the test is over. Glasses are identified by means of random numbers. You can make these up yourself (the task is not as simple as it sounds) or you can use the random numbers given in the preceding chapter.

Because a person *adapts* (loses the ability to catch nuances) quite quickly to certain stimuli, particularly to odors, a minimum of five minutes rest should be scheduled between the completion of one test and the start of another.

Since approximately two ounces of wine are to be poured into a glass for judging, a fifth bottle will suffice for 10 to 12 glasses, leaving a small reserve for possible retasting. If more wine of a single kind is needed for a specific test, buy all the needed bottles from the same store and, if possible, from the same case. Then, before you actually make use of them, *blend them together* so that you will, have exactly the same wine as a base throughout the test. In many cases, you may find it preferable to buy wine in a half gallon or gallon jug. (Unfortunately, it is almost impossible to find a varietal wine in these larger containers.)

Red wines should be served at what is generally called "room temperature", the assumption being that the room is not excessively warm. A red wine probably tastes best at about 60° to 65°, while most people probably feel best with the room temperature at 70° to 75°. When a room is around 75°—and certainly when it is warmer—I feel it would do a red wine no harm to have a few minutes in the refrigerator before it is actually poured. Some of my confreres disagree with this stand.

White wines are generally served chilled (see footnote, page 29). If, as can happen, the wine reaches the tasting table a trifle too cold for the judge to get the full aroma and bouquet, he can resolve this readily by warming the glass bowl in his cupped hands.

Except on such occasions, wine glasses are generally held by the stem in judging, though some judges clamp the base between thumb and forefinger.

The tests described in the coming chapters are, as noted before, of two kinds. In the first section, you will find a number of tests intended to help you measure your capacity to discriminate among wines containing varying amounts of specific components. Following this is a section concerned with your capacity for judging wines *en toto*.

While to this point I have been exclusively concerned—just as you have been—with "you" and "your" judging capacity, from now on I will be blending in talk about a "judge" and a judge's capacity. This becomes necessary because certain preparations have to be made for each test and the person who makes these preparations cannot at the same time be the one who takes the tests. If it is you who are to be making the judgments (presumably with some companions), then it will have to be someone else who does the necessary blending, numbering, serving and scoring. Conversely, if you do the preparatory work, it must be others who take the tests.

If, as I hope, the tests will be taken by a group—it's much more fun that way—it seems to me that it would be interesting to get an idea beforehand of the taste similarities or dissimilarities of the members of such a group.

One way to do so that comes to mind—and I'm sure it's unscientific but I can't come up with anything better—is to present the group, sometime in advance of the actual judgings, with four wines of the same general type but with distinctive differences among them and ask each group member to record which he liked best, next best, third best and least. The wines should, of course, be offered blind so that no one is influenced by a brand name.[†]

◆ ◆ ◆

[†]*Editor's Note: See Appendix for Suggested Wines for Comparison.*

Chapter 14

LEARNING TO RECOGNIZE DIFFERENCES IN INDIVIDUAL TASTE COMPONENTS

The tests described in this section are designed to help measure ability to recognize a wine as having more or less of one or another of four major taste components. The components to be covered by these tests are sweetness, acidity, tannin and volatile acidity (vinegariness), sometimes called *acescence*. There are a number of volatile acids in wine, but acetic acid and its companion ester, ethel acetate, which gives the pronounced vinegar smell and taste, dominate in their effect on the senses.

There are two kinds of tests involved here. The first presents the person who is to make the judgments with a series of five sets of two glasses each and requires him to decide which glass in each set contains the wine that has *more* of the particular component for which his sensitivity is being tested.

The second kind is a single-shot affair for each component. Here, the judge is confronted with a set of four glasses, with each glass known to contain a different amount of a specified component, and is asked to line up the glasses according to the strength of this component.

In addition to these two types of tests, I have included a sort of graduation examination, in which a series of single, glasses is offered for comparison with a base wine and the judge is asked to state in each case which of the four components (sweetness, acidity, tannin, vinegariness) has been augmented in the proffered glass.

Preparation of the wines for the above tests is outlined in the following chapter. The blending ratios used offer component variations that are only slightly less difficult to recognize than those used by the University of California Department of Viticulture and Enology in giving tests to measure budding professional capacities.

These tests are therefore not child's play. If they don't measure wine judging capacities at the professional level, they certainly do so at the level of a promising connoisseur.

Because of this, it is important to take into account the general level of wine knowledge of the individuals who are to take these tests.

For experienced wine lovers, the given proportions should stand (though there may be times when you will want to make them more stringent). For those with lesser experience, the indicated proportions can be increased in relation to your estimate of the tasters' abilities.

In the two-glass series, assuming the component variations fit the judges' backgrounds, four correct answers out of five warrant a passing grade. In the four-glass lineup, the only acceptable error for a passing grade is that of transposing the positions of two glasses that properly belong next to each other (i.e.: reversing positions 2 and 3 to 3 and 2).

Either white or red wine can be used for these tests, though a rosé is preferable when tannin is the component being evaluated. The wine need not, and perhaps should not, be of strong varietal character. A popular priced generic wine (Chablis, Sauterne, Claret, Burgundy) in gallons or half gallons provides a base wine that makes a good control for these tests because it generally does not have an overwhelming character.* The use of one of these larger containers also makes economic sense since the per-ounce cost is lower than for wines purchased in fifths.†

A half gallon will serve up to 32 glasses, using 2 oz. of wine per glass, though this leaves no reserve for retasting. A half gallon is thus enough to put one individual through three of the 2-glass series or three persons through one such series. In the four-glass test, a half gallon will serve eight judges per component, should you have the space or the inclination to involve yourself to that extent.

---

*However, a sweet Sauterne is not recommended as the base wine for measuring sensitivity to sweetness.

†*Editor's Note:* If you are buying your wine in bottles versus gallons, one gallon of wine is equivalent to a little over five 750 mL bottles of wine (a half-gallon is 2.5 750 mL bottles).

The use of this amount of wine is not as wasteful as it may seem at first since much of the wine remains in its original state and can be consumed later by the individual taster or tasters. Or, following the pattern pursued by one friend, the contents of selected glasses can later be poured together in optional proportions, resulting in self-blended wines that are sometimes more interesting than the originals.

Generally, no more than two components should be tested during an evening. To do more would require so many glasses, take up so much space and involve so much time as to discourage the taking of subsequent tests.

An interesting combination to be tasted in a single evening is that of acidity and sweetness. This is so because, after the tests are over, the wines can be combined (low acid with low sugar, high acid with high sugar and vice versa) in varying proportions to show how the definiteness of each component on the taste buds is affected by the presence of the other.

Is it possible, you may ask, in dealing with as complex a product as wine, to set the mind and the senses to measuring a single component while forcing the other components into a mental and sensory background?

Yes, it's possible. But it requires concentration and practice.

You may find it difficult at first to make such selective measurements with wine, but there is plenty of evidence you can do so with other complexities involving sensory evaluation.

Example: You're listening to a symphony with the sounds of many strings, woodwinds, reed instruments, brasses and tympanies all beautifully balanced to make an ear-satisfying whole. Then you decide you want to concentrate on the violins. In surprising detail, you catch the sound of the fiddles even when they are merely being supportive of other instruments.

Example: You are served a delicious soup in a restaurant. You are enjoying it as a delightful whole when someone in your party says, "Can you recognize the touch of thyme in the soup?" and suddenly, because you concentrate on it, the taste of thyme comes through to you even though you were not previously conscious of it.

These examples assume that you already know what a violin sounds like and what thyme tastes like. You are not likely to be as well acquainted with some of the components you will be dealing with in trying to make sensory evaluations of wine. But with each effort in this direction your eyes, nose and taste buds should become more familiar with the separate components and sooner or later you should find yourself capable of making judgments on at least some of them selectively. The purpose of the tests presented in this section is to give you practice in making such selective judgments.

In describing these tests, I have quite possibly over-explained each step. This has been done because some individuals prefer to follow explicit directions. If this is not the way you operate, simply look over the described steps to get the general idea and then proceed on your own in whatever manner suits you.

◆ ◆ ◆

Chapter 15

PREPARING THE WINES FOR COMPONENT TESTING

Preparing wines for component tests calls for overloading them with varying amounts of a particular component. (My term, "overloading", evolves from the belief that the base wine was component-balanced by the winemaker.)

To achieve this end, a solution is first prepared according to formula, after which measured amounts of the solution are added to the wine.

Assuming that 2 oz. (a quarter cup) of wine will be used per glass per judge (the recommended amount), simple arithmetic will provide you with the amount of component-overloaded blend or blends you will need for each test. These can be prepared a day or so beforehand (with the exception of the tannin blends, which should be readied just before tasting) and the wines can be kept refrigerated until needed. The red wines should be removed from the refrigerator in time for them to reach room temperature before being offered for tasting. Empty wine bottles (fifths or tenths) with screw caps can be used as storage vessels.

The blending pattern to be followed with each of the components is described below, first for the 4-Step Lineup tests and then for the Paired Comparison tests.

PREPARING BLENDS FOR THE 4-STEP TESTS

The preparation of the blends discussed in this section involves, in each case, the making up of an intermediate solution of component and wine, then using this solution to produce the required three blends (the fourth step being that of the base wine alone).

Sweetness. Use cane sugar, not powdered sugar. An added glass or other container is needed in making the sugared blends in order to pour the sweetened wine from one vessel to another until the sugar is completely dissolved.

To make the solution, dissolve a teaspoon of sugar per 3 oz. of wine required (allow a minimum of 1 oz. of solution per judge). Use this solution to prepare the blends in the following proportions:

Light Sweet . . . . .1 teaspoon for every 2 oz. wine.
Medium Sweet. . . . . .2 teaspoons for every 2 oz. wine.
Very Sweet. . . . . .1 tablespoon for every 2 oz. wine.

These blends may be prepared ahead of time and kept in clearly marked containers.

Total Acid. Dissolve $1/4$ teaspoon Citric Acid into 5 oz. of the base wine. Use this solution to make three wine blends in the following proportions:

Light Acid . . . . .1 teaspoon per 2 oz. wine.
Medium Acid. . . . . .2 teaspoons per 2 oz. wine.
High Acid . . . . .1 tablespoon per 2 oz. wine.

These blends may be prepared ahead of time and kept in clearly marked containers.

Volatile Acid. Blend 1 tablespoon of distilled vinegar of 5% acidity (check the label) into 5 oz. of wine. You will need 3 oz. of this solution per judge. Use this solution to make three blends in the following proportions:

Light Acetic . . . . .1 teaspoon per 2 oz. wine.
Medium Acetic . . . . .2 teaspoons per 2 oz. wine.
High Acetic . . . . .4 teaspoons per 2 oz. wine.

These blends may be prepared ahead of time and kept in clearly marked containers. The vinegar may be red if red wine is being used for the tests. However, white distilled vinegar serves the same purpose with red wine and is of course essential with white wine tests. It is not necessary (but is better) to use a wine vinegar.

Tannin. Dissolve $1/4$ teaspoon of Tannic Acid[†] into 9 oz. of wine, allowing 2 oz. of this solution for each judge. Use this solution to make three wine blends in the following proportions:

Light Tannin . . . . .1 teaspoon per 3 oz. wine.
Medium Tannin. . . . . .2 teaspoons per 3 oz. wine.
High Tannin . . . . .4 teaspoons per 3 oz. wine.

Do NOT prepare these tannic acid solutions ahead of time. Tannic acid tends to hydrolyze to gallic acid with the passage of time and gallic acid can be toxic. As an added safety measure, the judges should be warned not to swallow these samples but to spit them out.

Even though you will be preparing these tannin blends just before the tests are to take place, mark each container clearly for identification.

PREPARING BLENDS FOR PAIRED COMPONENT TESTING

In contrast to the need for readying multi-blends for the four-step tests above, it is necessary here merely to prepare blends for single-step comparisons per component. Since the judge is required only to decide which of two glasses offered him at a time contains the wine that is stronger in a particular component, the extent to which a wine should be overloaded for this single step test is subject to a certain leeway. This involves your assessment of the experience of the judge or judges. While newcomers to wine judging can sometimes do as well as experienced tasters in simple component tests, in general the greater the wine knowledge of the judges the smaller should be the component differences among the wines offered them. I therefore feel some differentiation should be made on the basis of wine experience.

[†]*Editor's Note:* It is highly advisable that in lieu of tannic acid, you use brewed regular black tea to add tannins to wine for this application. Use ½ teaspoon of brewed tea per half-gallon of wine.

Following this concept and using the same preparatory patterns presented for the 4-step tests, the overloading of a wine for the paired tests should be made according to this guide:

Beginner: Match the blending pattern for the most overloaded wine in the 4-step preparations (*Very Sweet, High Acid, High Tannin, High Acetic*).

More Experienced: Match the pattern for the *Medium* blends in the 4-step preparations.

Connoisseur: Match the blending pattern for the *Light* blends in the 4-step preparations. With the exception of the tannin augmentation, the blends can be prepared a day beforehand and kept refrigerated until needed.

In contrast to the sequence in which the blending instructions have been presented, it is better to begin the actual judgings with the 2-step tests before undertaking the presentation of the 4-step tests. The following chapters present the tests in this preferred sequence.

◆ ◆ ◆

Chapter 16

THE 2-STEP COMPONENT TESTS

GENERAL IDEA: A judge is presented with a series of two wines and is asked to select the wine which is stronger in a particular component (sweetness, total acidity, tannin, volatile acidity). The component being sought is made known to the judge.

REQUIRED:

- A base wine and a component-blended wine, the latter prepared according to the directions in the preceding chapter.
- Ten glasses per judge for each component to be offered.
- The usual control sheet, scorecards, counters, measuring and marking devices.
- The usual bread or crackers, cheese, glass of water, spittoon.

Because this is the first series of tests to be presented in this booklet, there have been included here a table and a graph that should help clarify the preparatory set-ups for these tests and for the non-graphed tests to follow.

PREPARATION

1. Pick any starting point on the chart of random numbers (Chapter 12) and select 10 successive numbers. (Ex.: starting at the top of column three and moving downward, the sequence of the selected numbers would be 20, 12, 64, 06, 44, 96, 78, 84, 34, 01.) As you pick out these numbers, pair them in vertical sequence on the control sheet:

20	12
64	06
44	96
78	84
34	01

2. Mark ten glasses per judge with the selected numbers and line up each set of ten on the work table in the same order as shown on the control sheet. Assuming three judges, this is what the line up of glasses should look like:

3. The next step is to establish randomly which glass (left or right) of each set is to receive the overloaded wine, that containing the augmented taste component. Write "Left" on three counters and "Right" on another three. Place the counters in a bowl and mix thoroughly. Blindly select one counter. If it says "Left", place a "0" (for "Overloaded") around the left hand number of the first of the control sheet's paired numbers (in this case, 20). Repeat this maneuver for the other four paired numbers. You will end up with one unused counter in the bowl (discard) and with the left file of paired numbers

carrying either two or three circles—circles which, remember, represent the overloaded wine.

4. Prepare the scorecards (one for each judge) leaving space at the top for the judge's names. Assuming the test is for sweetness, write down the instructions: *You will be presented with a series of five sets of two glasses each. One glass in each set will contain wine which is sweeter* than its mate. You are to circle the number of the wine that is SWEETER**. Below, copy the paired numbers from the control sheet in their exact sequence. Do NOT reproduce the identifying circles.

5. Measure out 2 oz. (a quarter cup) of the base wine into each glass whose number on the control sheet is NOT circled. This operation is simplified by the fact that the position of the numbered glasses on the work table matches that of the numbers on the control sheet. Check to see no errors have been made.

6. Measure out and pour a quarter cup of the overloaded wine into each of the remaining glasses.

THE TEST

With the tasting table set up and with the judges seated and ready, bring on the scorecards and ask each judge to write his name at the top. Read the instructions and answer any questions. (One question you will likely encounter: "Will all sets of glasses contain the same two wines?" The answer of course is "Yes".)

•   Bring on the first pair of glasses. Five minutes should be sufficient for the 2-glass test. Remove the first set and bring on the second. Repeat until all five sets have been judged.

•   Pick up the scorecards, take them into the working area and check them against the control sheet. This is simplified by the fact that you need only match circle with circle. Because of the element of chance, three correct answers are hardly worthy of

---

*Or "more acidic", "more tannic", "more vinegary", according to the particular test.

praise. Four indicate a fair ability and five correct replies warrant a pat on the back.

- Return the scorecards to the judges and encourage open discussion. If any judge wants to retaste a specific set of two glasses, allow him to do so.

Note: In the test for tannin content, advise the judges not to swallow the proffered wines.

◆ ◆ ◆

Chapter 17

THE 4-STEP
COMPONENT TESTS

GENERAL IDEA: A judge is presented with four glasses and is asked to line them up according to the strength of a specified component.

REQUIRED:

- A base wine and three blends of that wine, prepared according to the directions given in Chapter 15.
- Four glasses per judge.
- The usual control sheet, scorecards, counters, measuring and marking devices.
- The usual bread or crackers, cheese, water glass and pitcher, spittoon, tray.

PREPARATION

1. On the control sheet, under a heading of "Correct Sequence", put down in a horizontal line four random numbers, leaving space between them. Under each number, starting from the left, write one of the following *in sequence:* STRONG, MEDIUM, LIGHT, BASE. The lineup should look like this:

34	52	60	31
STRONG	MEDIUM	LIGHT	BASE

Lower down on the control sheet write another heading, "Presentation Sequence," in preparation for the next step.

2. Copy each of the random numbers and its companion word from the control sheet onto a counter. Place the four counters in a bowl, mix and select one blindly. Write its number and descriptive word under and to the left of the "Presentation

Sequence" heading on the Control Sheet. In turn, select the other three counters and copy their numbers and messages onto the Control Sheet, placing each in turn to the right of the preceding couplet. The lineup may now look like this:

60	34	31	52
LIGHT	STRONG	BASE	MEDIUM

3. Mark four glasses per judge with the random numbers and line up each set of four on the work table, *following the exact numerical pattern shown by the presentation sequence* on the control sheet.

4. Bring out the base wine and the blends and pour. The presentation sequence tells you what wine goes in what glass (pour 2 oz., a quarter cup, per glass).

5. Prepare the scorecards. Leaving room at the top for the judges' names, write down instructions: *You will be presented with four glasses of wine. You are to line up the glasses (left to right) according to the strength of their sweetness.* List the wines by number in sequence.* Under the instructions, draw four dash rules in line.

THE TEST

•   Distribute the scorecards and have the judges write their names at the top. Read the instructions and answer any questions.

•   Bring on the sets of glasses, making certain in each case that they are placed before the judges *exactly as they stood on the work table.* Use of the tray simplifies this.

•   Allow 15 minutes for the test. Leaving the glasses on the table, collect the scorecards and check them against the control sheet. One transposition of two juxtaposed numbers (31-60 when the proper sequence is 60-31) gives the judge, if not a pat on the back, at least a passing grade.

◆ ◆ ◆

---

*Or "acidity", "tannin content", "vinegariness", according to the particular test.

Chapter 18

PICKING THE UNKNOWN COMPONENT

GENERAL IDEA: A judge is given time to become acquainted with a wine, which remains available for re-tasting. He is then presented with a series of six single glasses containing the same wine made sweeter, more acidic, more tannic or more vinegary. He is asked to identify the specific component that has been augmented in each glass.

REQUIRED:

- A sound generic wine with good balance.
- Sugar, tannic acid, citric acid, vinegar.
- Seven glasses for each judge.
- The usual scorecards, control sheet, counters, measuring and marking devices.
- The usual bread and crackers, cheese, water glass and pitcher, spittoon, tray.

PREPARATION

1. List six random numbers vertically on the Control Sheet. Circle one of the numbers haphazardly.

2. Using eight counters, write each of the following on two counters: *Sweeter, More Vinegary, More Tannic, More Acidic.*

3. Place the counters in a bowl, mix thoroughly and blindly select one. Write its message opposite the first number on the control sheet. In turn, select the five other counters, the message from each being placed *in turn* against one of the random numbers.

4. This leaves two unused counters in the bowl. Discard these *unless they both say the same thing* (which means that the component

change shown by these counters is not represented on the control sheet). The solution: substitute the message shown by these counters for that previously placed against the circled random number on the control sheet.

5. Mark six glasses per judge with the random numbers from the control sheet (the 7th glass per set is for the base wine and is left unmarked). Line up all six-glass sets in the order shown on the Control Sheet.

6. Ready the scorecards. Leaving room at top for the judges' names, write down instructions: *You will be given time to become acquainted with a wine, which will remain before you for re-tasting as you desire. Six glasses will then be brought you one at a time. These glasses will contain the base wine, modified so as to make it sweeter, more acidic, more tannic or more vinegary. You are to judge in which way the wine has been changed. You must make a decision even if it is only a guess. There will be duplications.* Below, in vertical sequence, put down the random numbers as shown on the control sheet, placing a dash rule opposite each.

READYING THE BLENDS

The following instructions are based on the understanding that each glass is to contain approximately 2 oz. (a quarter cup) of wine. Thus, with each component, the amount of wine to be prepared depends on two things—the number of judges and whether the particular taste augmentation (Ex.: *Sweeter*) appears on the control sheet once or twice. If, for example, there are to be three judges and *Sweeter* is shown twice on the control sheet (equal to six judging opportunities) this calls for the sweetening of 12 oz. (1 $^1/_2$ cups) of wine.

With the exception of the required tannin blends, the component-augmented wines may be prepared ahead of time. White wines can be refrigerated. Empty fifth or tenth bottles with screw caps can be used as containers. Mark each container for identification.

To make the blends, keep in mind the abilities of those taking the test. Use the blending proportions shown in Chapter 15, beginning on page 65. For the *beginner*, match the blending pattern for the most overloaded wine (Very Sweet, High Acid, High Tannin, High Acetic). For the *more experienced*, match the pattern for the medium blends. And for the *connoisseur*, match the pattern for the lightest blends.

THE TEST

- Following the dictates of the control sheet, pour the augmented wines from the separate containers into the numbered glasses, using a quarter cup to measure out the required 2 oz. per glass. Into the seventh (unnumbered) glass of each set pour the base wine.

- Bring the unmarked glasses to the judges' table and distribute the scorecards. After the judges have written their names on the cards, read the instructions aloud and answer any questions.

- Allow the tasters time to become acquainted with the base wine, then bring on the first of the numbered glasses. After five minutes (or before, if all judges are finished), remove this glass and bring on the second in order. Follow this pattern until all glasses have been tasted. (The removed glasses should be returned to their former positions on the work table to permit retasting after the test is over should the judges so desire.)

- When the final round of numbered, glasses has been distributed and evaluated, collect the scorecards and check the judges' decisions against those on the Control Sheet. Or if you prefer, simply call out the correct answers and have the judges correct their own cards. Either way, when the cards are all marked, encourage open discussion. Five correct identifications out of the six attempts can be taken to indicate a substantial ability to recognize component differences—at least for these four components.

◆ ◆ ◆

WINE EVALUATION TESTS

Chapter 19

INTRODUCTION TO TOTAL WINE TASTE-TESTING

This is as far along the road of component evaluation as I can take you. I regret that the previously listed tests encompass only four components, important as they are, but whenever I tried a new avenue seeking a test for some other component, I invariably came across an outsized sign that read "Dead End". Nevertheless, I would like to make a few additional comments regarding this aspect of learning to judge wines.

There are, I admit, tests for measuring sensitivity to various *odors*. How soundly based they are, I don't know, but I have watched people undergo such testing. The difficulty is that the tests require complicated laboratory equipment and must be administered under controlled conditions by trained personnel. There was no way I could see in which such testing procedures could be successfully simplified for your home use.[†]

As regards *color*, there seems to be no practical test to measure your ability to know when a particular wine is within its proper color range. However, if your only concern is to test your own or someone else's sensitivity to color change, you can do so by (1) pouring a couple of ounces of wine into each of four randomly numbered glasses, then (2) thinning the wine in three of the glasses with successively greater additions of water,[*] (3) mixing up the glasses after recording their proper sequence, and (4) asking the one doing the judging to line up the four glasses in the order of their color intensity.

[†]Editor's Note: Wine aroma kits are available for one to train their sense of smell by recognizing and identifying common smells and terms used to describe aromas in wine tasting.

[*]But subsequently levelling off the amount of liquid in each glass to keep from providing a clue.

Designing a test that would measure your ability to evaluate the *flavor* of a wine is beyond my capacity and, from what I gather, beyond the capacity of anyone else unless it's for someone who already possesses enough background experience to recognize what flavor a particular type of wine should have. In such a case, as I see it, such an individual would have little need for this kind of test.

Tests for *body* in wine? I've already taken this up but to repeat: Those with whom I've conferred about this say tests for such a purpose cannot be concocted in any scientific or value-producing way. I suppose if you took, a wine you considered to have a heavy body and thinned it out in steps (as with the color test above) you would have a test of sorts. Only what would be the measure of its validity?[†]

With the above considerations in mind, this seems to be a good spot at which to leave behind those tests aimed at helping you learn to recognize varying amounts of a specific component in a wine and to go forward to those tests concerned with helping you judge wine as a complex of a great number of components.

The tests offered in these final chapters are substantially more sophisticated than those you've been confronted with to this point. Even if they are not the ultimate among tests used to evaluate the capacity of an individual to be a professional wine judge, they are considered to be sufficiently advanced to establish those who complete the series with high scores as having earned a mark of "excellent" in the field of amateur wine judging.

Let me repeat my earlier statement regarding what you may consider the excessive particularization of the way to prepare and run the tests—each test is headed by a short paragraph

---

[†]*Editor's Note:* While there may be lack of agreement on what constitutes "body" in wine or what the agreed position is on necessary conditions of "fullness", there is a widespread understanding amongst experienced wine tasters that body is an important feature in distinguishing differences between wines. A study conducted by the Australian Wine Research Institute found that wine tasters tend to strongly correlate flavor and perceived viscosity (versus acidity, hotness from alcohol or glycerol) with fullness of a wine and therefore these two attributes were part of their interpretation of the term 'body'. It should be noted that this study was conducted using only white wines.

outlining its set-up and purpose. This may prove to be sufficient for you to go off on your own in getting the test ready and in administering it. If so, fine. However, the step-by-step program is there if you need it.

A final word: The upcoming tests may seem to be very similar in concept but each is calculated to measure tasting capacity in a different way and the sequence in which the tests are presented provides increasingly severe measures of judging capacity.

◆ ◆ ◆

Chapter 20

TEST 1: YES IT IS; NO IT ISN'T

GENERAL IDEA: A wine is offered for acquaintanceship, remaining available for retasting. The judge is then asked to identify a series of glasses offered him one at a time as containing or not containing the original wine.

REQUIRED:

- A wine with definite character (Wine "A") and at least one different wine ("B").
- Six glasses per judge.
- The usual Control Sheet, scorecards, counters, measuring and marking devices.
- The usual bread or crackers, cheese, water glass and pitcher, spittoon, tray.

PREPARATION

1. On the Control Sheet, put down in columnar form five random numbers.

2. Write "Same" on three counters and "Different" on another three. Place the counters in a bowl and blindly select one. Copy its message onto the Control Sheet against the first listed number. Repeat in sequence with the remaining counters until all five numbers on the Control Sheet have notations opposite them. Discard the last (sixth) counter.

3. Line up five glasses per judge on the work table and number each set of five in the sequence shown by the Control Sheet. The sixth glass per judge remains unmarked and is placed so that it will be the first glass offered.

4. Ready the scorecards. Leaving room at the top for the judges' names, type out the instructions: *You will be given a wine to*

taste for the purpose of later recognition. Subsequently, you will be given a series of five glasses one at a time and in each case asked to identify the wine in the glass as either being the wine originally tasted or as not being that wine. Your decision, "Same" or "Different," is to be written against the number below that matches the number on the glass. Below the instructions, duplicate in columnar form the list of random numbers from the control sheet.

THE TEST

- Give each taster his scorecard and ask him to write his name at the top. Read the instructions aloud and answer any questions regarding tasting procedure.

- Bring in the unmarked glasses with the base wine and give the judges a few minutes to become acquainted with it. Now bring in the first of the numbered glasses and when the judges have made their decisions on this wine, remove the glasses and, again after a short pause, bring in the second set. Continue in this fashion until all five glasses have been tasted and all decisions recorded.

- Collect the scorecards and check the decisions against the control sheet, marking the wrong answers.* Because guesses can be responsible on a fifty-fifty basis for a correct answer on each wine, four of the five replies should be correct to warrant a mark of "good".

- If the judges so desire, bring back the previously removed numbered glasses to allow re-comparisons on incorrect identifications.

Note: This test can be made more difficult if, instead of having only one alternative wine ("B"), two or three different wines are used.

◆ ◆ ◆

___

*As an alternative throughout the tests in this section, you can let the judges correct their own cards as you read the answers from the control sheet.

Chapter 21

TEST 2: THIS IS IT

GENERAL IDEA: A wine is presented for acquaintanceship, remaining available for retasting throughout test. Five sets of paired glasses are then served in turn, with one glass in each set known to contain the wine originally tasted. The judge is asked to select the glass in each set containing the originally tasted wine. (This is a variant of the preceding test but with identification made a bit more difficult by the presence of a second wine.)

REQUIRED:

- Two wines, red or white, of quite similar character. (The closer the two wines come to matching, the more difficult the identification.)
- Eleven glasses for each judge.
- The usual control sheet, scorecards, counters, measuring and marking devices.
- The usual bread or crackers, cheese, water glass and pitcher, spittoon, tray.

PREPARATION

1. Mark the bottle containing the wine to be offered as the original wine with an "O".
2. On the control sheet, put down in columnar form five paired sets of random numbers.
3. For each judge, number, pair and place ten glasses on the work table, duplicating the pattern shown on the control sheet. In front of each set of ten glasses, place an unmarked glass.
4. Write "Left" on three counters and "Right" on another three. Place the counters in a bowl, mix and, one by one, select five counters. With each selection, circle in vertical sequence the

right or left hand number of the paired numbers on the control sheet, according to the dictates of the counter. Discard the remaining counter.

5. Pour 2 oz. (quarter cup) of the original wine into one of each pair of glasses, as indicated by the *circled* number on the Control Sheet. Also pour this wine into the unmarked glass standing before each set of ten. Check to see no errors have been made. Pour 2 oz. of the second wine into all remaining empty glasses.

6. Prepare the scorecards. Leave room at the top for the judges' names, then write down instructions: *You will be given a wine* to taste which remains available for retasting. Later you will be offered five sets of paired glasses. You are to circle the number of the glass in each set which contains the wine you originally tasted.* Below this, copy the five sets of paired numbers from the Control Sheet.

THE TEST

• Distribute the scorecards and have each judge place his name at the top. Read the instructions aloud and answer pertinent questions.

• Bring on the unmarked glasses containing the "original" wine and allow five minutes for the judges to become acquainted with it.

• At appropriate intervals, bring on the series of paired glasses for identification.

• Leaving the last set of glasses on the table, collect the score sheets and check them against the control sheet. Because of the element of guesswork, 4 correct answers are required to warrant a passing grade here.

• Return the scorecards to the judges and encourage open discussion. Permit retasting if desired.

◆ ◆ ◆

---

*If you want to make this a test of varietal identification, name the wine type being offered.

Chapter 22

TEST 3: PAIRED COMPARISONS

GENERAL IDEA: The judge is presented with a series of paired glasses and in each case is asked if there is a difference between the two wines in each set.

REQUIRED:

- Two wines of the same general type but with measurable differences. The ability of the judges should be considered in selecting the wines; the more experienced the judges, the more alike the wines should be.
- Fourteen glasses per judge.
- The usual control sheet, scorecards, counters, measuring and marking devices.
- The usual bread or crackers, cheese, water glass and pitcher, spittoon, tray.

PREPARATION

1. Mark bottles of wine as "A" and "B".
2. On the control sheet, put down seven sets of paired random numbers, leaving space after each number for later alphabetic identification.
3. Line up glasses on work table in paired rows (one set for each judge) and mark them in sequence with the numbers from the control sheet.
4. Prepare the scorecards. Leaving room at the top for judges' names, put down instructions: *You will be presented in turn with seven sets of paired glasses and will be asked to determine if the wine in the two glasses is the same or different. Only two wines are being used in this test and either wine may be duplicated in any set. Below,*

in vertical file, copy the seven sets of paired numbers from the control sheet.

5. On each of four counters write one of the following alphabetic combinations: A-A; A-B; B-A; B-B." Duplicate with another four counters. Place the eight counters in a bowl and mix.*

6. Blindly select one counter and copy its alphabetical sequence onto the control sheet, placing each letter in turn against one of the first paired numbers (Ex.: 74-A; 16-B). In this manner, select a total of seven counters and in sequence record their alphabetic order against the numerical pairs on the control sheet. Discard the remaining counter.

7. On the control sheet, against each set of paired numbers, write "Same" or "Different" to reflect the alphabetical pairings.

8. Following the control sheet, pour 2 oz. (quarter cup) of Wine "A" into all glasses whose numbers correspond to those on the control sheet marked by "A." Check to see no errors have been made, then pour Wine "B" into the remaining empty glasses.

THE TEST

• Give each judge his scorecard and have him write his name at the top. Read the instructions and answer questions that may arise.

• Bring on the first set of paired wines. Immediately when all judges are through (no need for delay here since no taste memory is involved), remove the glasses and bring on the next set. Continue through the seven sets.

• Collect the scorecards and check them against the control sheet. Because chance can enter into the judgments, five correct answers is a bare passing, six promising and seven, of course, perfect.

---

*While A-B and B-A are in a sense duplicates, there is involved the psychological effect of the two wines being presented in a different order.

(One learned researcher who checked this material said he does not believe seven tests offer a statistically sound basis for evaluating the capacity of a judge to differentiate between two wines. His suggested minimum: eight to ten paired sets. He is probably right in terms of professional evaluation of wines but in order to keep the test within reasonable bounds for home experimentation, I believe that seven sets of paired glasses are sufficient.)

Chapter 23

TEST 4: ODD MAN OUT

GENERAL IDEA: The judge is presented with a series of 3-glass sets, with two of the glasses in each set known to contain the same wine. The judge is to select the odd sample.

REQUIRED:

- Two wines similar in character, but with the extent of their similarity depending on the experience of the judge or judges making up the tasting panel.
- Fifteen glasses per judge.
- The usual control sheet, scorecards, counters, marking and measuring devices.
- The usual bread or crackers, cheese, water glass and pitcher, spittoon, tray.

PREPARATION

1. Mark one bottle of wine "A" and the other "B".
2. On the control sheet, write down in column form five sets of three random numbers. Below each set of three numbers, draw a line to separate it from the following set.
3. On the work table, copy the random numbers from the Control Sheet onto 15 glasses per judge, keeping each group of 15 glasses in the same numerical order and the same 3-glass set sequence as on the control sheet.
4. Ready the scorecards. Leaving room for the judges' names at the top, write down the following instructions: *Five sets of three glasses each will be served to you in sequence. Two of each set of three glasses will contain the same wine, the third glass will contain a different wine. The same two wines will be used throughout the test. In each case, write down the number of the glass containing the DIFFERENT*

wine. Below the instructions, write down in column form "Test 1", "Test 2", etc., each followed by a short dash rule.

5. On each of six counters write one of the following alphabetical sequences (with no duplications): A-A-B; A-B-B; B-A-A; B-B-A; B-A-B; A-B-A. Place the counters in a bowl and mix thoroughly. Blindly select one counter and copy its sequence of letters onto the control sheet, placing each letter in turn against one of the random numbers in the first numerical set. To clarify, assuming the counter reads "A-A-B" and the first three numbers are 47, 39 and 84, you would have the following:

47-A   39-A   84-B

In turn select four more counters and transpose the letters to the control sheet in the pattern delineated above. You will be left with one unused counter. Discard.

6. Pick up Bottle "A" and pour 2 oz. (quarter cup) into each glass whose corresponding number on the control sheet is followed by an "A". (Ex.: glasses 47 and 39 in *all* first sets of three glasses.) Check to make sure you have made no mistakes, then pick up Bottle "B" and pour into all remaining glasses.

THE TEST

• Distribute the scorecards and have the judges write their names at the top. Read the instructions and answer any questions.

• Bring on the first set of glasses. Allow five minutes for judging. Remove the first set of glasses and bring on the second. Follow this pattern until all five sets have been tasted.

• Collect the scorecards and check each against the control sheet, marking the wrong answers. Four correct answers rate a mark of "Good."

• Return the graded sheets to the judges, mentioning any oddities discovered in checking the sheets (Ex.: all failed to get the correct answer on the third set). Encourage open discussion, with particular emphasis on the major difference or differences the judges found in the two wines.

◆ ◆ ◆

Chapter 24

TEST 5: DOUBLE TROUBLE

GENERAL IDEA: The judge is presented with two wines as standards and is permitted time to establish the differences between them. Then, with the two wines always at hand for retasting, a series of paired wines is brought on and the judge is asked to match the unidentified samples with the two standards.

REQUIRED:

- Two wines, the differences between them depending on the experience of those doing the judging.
- Twelve glasses per judge.
- The usual control sheet, scorecards, counters, marking and measuring devices.
- The usual bread or crackers, cheese, water glass and pitcher, spittoon, tray.

PREPARATION

1. Mark the two wines "A" and "B".
2. On the control sheet, put down in column form 5 sets of paired random numbers, leaving space after each number for alphabetic identification. Haphazardly circle one pair of numbers.
3. Prepare the scorecards. Leaving, space at top for judges' names, write down instructions: *You will be presented with two wines ("A" and "B") and will be given time to establish the differences between them. These wines will remain available for retasting while a series of two unknown wines are offered for identification. Each wine must be identified as either "A" or "B", though the two wines need not be present simultaneously in anyone set. One pairing is duplicated.* Below this, list the five paired numbers from the control sheet, leaving plenty of room against each number for the judge to mark his alphabetic decision (or wine type name if this is what is being sought).

4. Copy the random numbers from the control sheet onto eight glasses per judge. Pair them on the worktable in the same order as on the control sheet. In front of each set place two glasses, marked "A" and "B".

5. Mark four counters in sequence as follows: A-A; A-B; B-A; B-B. Place in a bowl and mix thoroughly.

6. Blindly select one counter and copy the letters shown there against the first pair of numbers on the control sheet (Ex.: 43-A; 69-B). Repeat with the remaining three counters and the remaining paired numbers but skip the circled pair of numbers.

7. Now return the four counters to the bowl, mix again and select a single counter. Write its alphabetical sequence against the circled pair of numbers on the control sheet. Discard the counters.

8. Pour 2 oz. (quarter cup) of wine from Bottle "A" into all glasses whose numbers on the control sheet so designate. Also, pour the wine into the glass of each set marked "A". Check to see that there are no errors, then pour from Bottle "B" into all remaining glasses on the work table.

THE TEST

•   Distribute the scorecards and have the judges write their names at the top. Read the instructions and answer any questions.

•   Bring on the glasses marked "A" and "B" (or identified by wine type) and give the judges time (5 minutes) to acquaint themselves with the two. These wines remain throughout the test.

•   Bring on the first set of random numbered glasses and allow time for identification. Remove these and bring on the second set. Follow this pattern until all five sets have been judged.

•   Leaving the last set of glasses at the table, collect the scorecards and check the answers against the control sheet. Successful identification of four of the five sets can be considered very good.

•   Return scorecards and encourage open discussion. Permit retasting if so desired.

◆ ◆ ◆

Chapter 25
TEST 6: QUINTET LINE-UP

GENERAL IDEA: A judge is presented with a set of five glasses of wine and is asked to line the glasses up in the order of the varietal character of the wines they hold.

REQUIRED:

- Two wines of the same general classification but with one possessing definite varietal character, the other being of the same general type but with little or no varietal character. (Ex.: A top Pinot Noir and a "standard" Burgundy*.)[†]

- Six glasses per judge.

- The usual control sheet, scorecards, counters, marking and measuring devices.

- The usual bread or crackers, cheese, water glass and pitcher, spittoon.

PREPARATION

1. Designate the true varietal wine as "A", the other as "B".

2. On the control sheet, write down in columnar form five random numbers (Ex.: 84, 69, 71, 56, 75). Opposite each of these and *in the sequence shown below* list the wine-blending formula each number is to represent, as follows:

$$84 = 100\% \text{ Wine A.}$$

$$69 = 75\% \text{ Wine A} + 25\% \text{ Wine B.}$$

$$71 = 50\% \text{ Wine A} + 50\% \text{ Wine B.}$$

---

*Other combinations: Cabernet Sauvignon and Claret, Chardonnay and Chablis, Semillon and Sauterne, Johannisberg Riesling and Rhine.

[†]*Editor's Note:* If you are looking for a "standard" or entry-level Burgundy, they will not have a specific vineyard or appellation associated with them, and often carry a varietal designation such as a "Bourgogne Pinot Noir."

$$56 = 25\% \text{ Wine A} + 75\% \text{ Wine B.}$$

$$75 = 100\% \text{ Wine B.}$$

Well below this on the sheet, put down a heading: "Presentation Sequence."

3. Copy the random numbers onto five counters. Place the counters in a bowl, mix and select one. Transfer the number from this counter onto the control sheet under the "Presentation Sequence" heading, placing it to the *left* of the page. In turn, select the other four counters and in turn list each number to the right of the preceding number. This provides a pattern for the random presentation of the glasses.

4. For each judge, mark five glasses with the random numbers and line them up on the work table *in the order shown by the Presentation Sequence*. In front of each set of five glasses place one unmarked glass.

5. Using the above formulas, prepare the blends. To determine quantity, count 2 oz. (quarter cup) of each blend for each judge. Place each blend in a separate container and mark for identification. The two non-blends (100% A and 100% B) can remain in their original bottles.

6. From bottle "A" pour 2 oz. of wine into the unmarked glass in each set. This is to become the varietal glass by which the wine in the numbered glasses are to be judged.

7. Again from the bottle "A", pour 2 oz. of wine into the glass in each set whose number on the control sheet calls for 100% "A" (in the listing above, this would mean each glass numbered 84). Follow the same procedure with bottle "B" (for glasses numbered 75 above) and then follow up by pouring the three blends in turn, following the dictates of the control sheet in matching glass number and blend.

8. Prepare the scorecards. Leaving room at the top for the judges' names, put down the instructions: *You will be offered a glass of Pinot Noir* for acquaintance which will remain available for retasting as desired. You will then be presented with five glasses of wine*

---

*Or whatever varietal wine is being used as the control.

which you are to line up in the order of their Pinot Noir* character. List the wines by number on the lines below, starting at the TOP with what you consider to be the wine with the strongest varietal character. Underneath, draw five short lines in a vertical column.

THE TEST

- Distribute the scorecards and have the judges write their names at the top. Read the instructions and answer questions.

- Bring in the unnumbered glasses containing the varietal wine (Wine "A") and allow five minutes for acquaintanceship. The glasses remain available for retasting throughout the test.

- Bring in the sets of five numbered glasses, placing the glasses of each set before the judge in the exact sequence as they stood on the work table. Allow twenty minutes for evaluation.

- Collect the scorecards and check them against the control sheet. If the only sequential error is the transposition of two glasses that belong next to each other (56–71 instead of 71–56), this warrants a passing grade.

- Return the scorecards. Explain how the wines were differentiated. Allow the judges, if they desire, to check the wines again, this time against the known sequence.

PASSING ALONG WHAT YOU'VE LEARNED

Chapter 26
THE BEST WAY TO DESCRIBE A WINE

Now that, hopefully, you have become more knowledgeable about wine, it may well be that your friends will be asking for your opinion of one or another of the wines you have tested. How are you to answer them?

Let's begin with the simplest possible answer—"I liked (didn't like) it."

When you say this, what sort of information about the wine are you passing on? Obviously, very little. Some would say none at all. So, unless you are directly asked if you liked the wine, forget this reply as one that offers a value judgment.

The next elucidative forward step does offer a judgment of the wine but only in the most general terms. The wine, you say, was "great," "good," "fair," or "poor," using these very words or synonyms. This will satisfy many listeners. It is, however, likely to be considered an inadequate evaluation by those more than casually interested in wine.

So let's take another step forward. Let's turn to those who are writers and lecturers about wine and see what words and phrases they use to describe a wine. Here, too, you will find wide use of generalties but they will normally be other than the "great" to "poor" grouping noted previously, and they will in most cases be bolstered by certain specifics regarding color, aroma, bouquet, body or taste. Below are some examples of the type of general evaluations used, taken from actual writings about wine in consumer magazines, with the interpretations mine.

Big: A full-bodied wine, either young or mature, usually high in alcohol content and rich in flavors. A "big" red wine is often high in tannin and thus capable of further development with aging. Unless otherwise qualified, "big" implies a favorable impression.

Pleasant: Not exceptional but possessing a certain appeal and average quality.

Sound: Without major faults, but without major virtues as well.

Honest: Without pretentions; carries connotations of being adequate for its type and of being reasonably priced.

Ordinary: Lacking any distinction to the point where disappointment is implied. Possibly a shade below "honest" and "sound."

Undeveloped: The potential is present but needs aging before it will assert itself. "Closed-in" and "dumb" are used to describe an undeveloped aroma.

Developed: Implies that an age-worthy wine has reached its full stage of maturity or its "peak plateau."

Past its Peak: A wine judged, as the result of previous tasting and experience, to have been a better wine in the past. "Over-the-hill" is similar, but both imply the wine once reached a peak or a place on the hill.

As noted above, these generalities are augmented by specifics. In the writings I checked, the specifics did not cover the full range called for by the tasting scoreboard reproduced in this book, being limited, presumably, to those evaluative factors which the writer found exceptional on either the plus or minus side. Here are a few examples of the terms used, again with my own explanations.

Nose: The combination of aroma and the bouquet of a wine. Used when tasters prefer not to try to differentiate between the two.

Character: Possessing definiteness of fragrance and taste to the degree where the wine is identifiable. Character relates to the wine's composition as in varietal character or to a regional distinction, as in Rutherford grown Cabernet Sauvignon. In either case, the character ranges from pronounced to subtle.

Complex: Containing several odors and taste sensations, but in an agreeable, attractive combination.

Simple: A one-dimensional wine thus lacking in complexity. It implies the taster anticipated more than was delivered.

Intense: A double-edged word based on the depth, richness, and concentration of the wine. Intense wines call attention to themselves, much like intense people. The character and personality is usually ingratiating, sometime grating.

Elegant: Complex wine with an understated, subtle appeal that opts for finesse rather than power. Restrained appears to be a synonym for elegant.

Crisp: Pleasantly tart and lively on the tongue due to high, but not excessive acidity.

Cloying: Excessively sweet, final impression. The sticky-sweet taste overrides all others. A negative word.

Finish: Essentially, the final impression of the wine's taste on the palate after it has been swallowed. It varies in nature (crisp, cloying, tannic, etc.) and in duration.

Those who write about wine for consumers sometimes add to their reasonably definitive words some which are more dramatic than explanatory. Recently, for example, I came across a description of a wine in which the writer called its bouquet "paltry" and its taste "fat." I believe I can, with a little stretch of the imagination, understand what the writer meant by a "paltry" bouquet but I must admit that a "fat" taste in wine is beyond me.[†]

In wine evaluation, as in all human communications, the ideal calls for words to carry specific meanings—and to mean the same things to both speaker and listener. As is true of most ideals, actuality falls somewhat short of the hoped-for goal. In describing a wine for example, you are not likely to find an audience—even an audience of one—which will interpret your every explanatory word the same way you do. This should not, however, stop you from using words that are as definitive as possible. Even if your listeners don't get the exact nuances you intend, they will nevertheless end up with a better "feel" for the wine than if you limit yourself to generalities.

So in this rather roundabout fashion we come to what can be considered an authoritative source for exact-as-possible descriptive words for wine—a lexicon prepared for use by industry professionals.

[†]*Editor's Note:* Today, the term "fat" is often used in describing wines and is understood to mean that a wine is full in body and flavor. This can be a positive characteristic but a wine that is considered "too fat" can be interpreted as having exaggerated fruity flavors that may be unpleasing, dull or lacking acidity.

Some years ago, in pursuit of clarity in describing wines at the professional level, California enologists and winemakers, working through Wine Institute's Technical Advisory Committee, put together what could be called a Dictionary of Wine Tasting Terms.[†] Shunning such esoteric words as "bold," "aggressive," "noble," used by romantics, they compiled a list of terms that were as narrowly interpretive of what was being described as the technicians could make them. A selection of terms from that list, with meanings paraphrased, follows. While you will likely find a number of the listed terms too narrowly definitive or too technical for your non-professional use, an understanding of them will nevertheless help you subconsciously in your efforts to describe a wine fully.

◆ ◆ ◆

[†]*Editor's Note:* The guide referenced in this chapter is no longer published by the California Wine Institute. However, the tasting terms included by the author are relevant and continue to be used in widespread application to wine tasting. Other respected resources for wine tasting terms beyond those included in this book include The Oxford Companion to Wine, Sotheby's Wine Encyclopedia, How to Taste (Jancis Robinson) and The Wine Aroma Wheel (A.C. Noble). See Appendix *Describing Aromas & Flavors.*

Chapter 27

GUIDELINES FROM THE PROFESSIONALS

The descriptive words for wine beginning on the next page have been selected from a mimeograph published by the California Wine Institute for use by that state's vintners and by judges at wine competitions. The reason for the preparation and dissemination of the mimeograph is clearly stated in a foreword:

"Wine tasting, as a production control technique, depends upon converting into words the impression created by the reaction of the wine on the taster's palate. In order that the one wine, tasted by several individuals, be reported in the same way by each, it is necessary that all of the tasters use the same words for the separate palate impressions the wine creates."

The listed terms presented here do not include all the descriptive words in the Wine Institute guide. They do include most of those which apply to table wines, with which this book is solely concerned. The table wine terms *not* included are those whose meanings are beyond my capabilities to paraphrase so as to provide you with more practical clues than those appearing in the mimeograph.

Consider, for example, the word *ullaged*. Its given meaning: "The odor acquired by table wines when left in partly filled casks for a long time." While this may provide a guideline for the experienced professional, I doubt that it would to you. So, since I could not translate this explanation into words that would help you recognize this particular odor, I left it (and certain others) out.

This points up one of the difficulties in using a professional source for interpretive words in describing a wine. The Wine Institute treatise properly presumes the professional can recognize a specific odor or taste for what it is, needing only to be guided in giving it the same name as do other professionals. The non-professional, on the other hand, usually needs to be told how to *recognize* the particular odor or taste before properly naming it. This is why the following definitions are, to a substantial extent, my own interpretations of the technologists' explanations.

The listed words are presented in the same sectional and sub-sectional pattern as that of the Wine Institute mimeograph.

APPEARANCE

Brilliant: Sparkling clear.

Clear: No visible solids but somehow lacking sparkling clarity.

Dull: A suggestion of haziness but without visible suspended material.

Cloudy: Definitely hazy or having visible suspended material.

Precipitated: Visible deposit but with wine above clear.

COLOR

The terms used in describing color are self explanatory but are inevitably subject to personal interpretation.

White Wines

Light Yellow; Straw Color: Almost watery. May be with or without a slight greenish tinge.

Medium Yellow: Approaching the color of undiluted lemon juice.

Light Gold: A rounding touch of gold in the yellow.

Medium Gold: A full, rounded, deep golden color.

Amber; Light Brown: A color fault; usually the result of excessive oxidation.

Red Wines

Pink; Rosé: Self-defined. Grenache Pink may have orange tint; with other pinks, this may indicate over-oxidation.

Light Red: Deeper than pink; lighter than "standard" red.

Medium Red: Unquestionably red but without purple tint.

Dark Red: Very deep color, frequently with purple overtones.

Tawny: Tinged with brown; a sign of age or over-oxidation.

AROMA

Varietal: Has smell characteristic of the predominant grape.

Distinct: Possesses individuality but not intensely enough to identify grape sources.

Vinous: Smells like a grape wine without any individuality.

BOUQUET

Cask-Aged: Possesses blend of odors reflecting wine was held in casks for proper period. Includes sensation of "oakiness."

Bottle-Aged: Possesses rounded balance of odors brought about by continued maturation in the bottle (important to recognize; impossible to describe).

OFF-ODORS

Off-odors are odors which are foreign to the normal smell of a clean sound wine. They may be just barely detectable or may dominate the sensation the nose gets. They are the result of unwanted changes in the maturing wine, brought about by a variety of factors. The first three listed below, for example, result from excess of sulfur-containing compounds:

Hydrogen Sulfide: Possesses the so-called "rotten egg" smell.

Sulfur Dioxide: Has a pungent smell, clearly suggestive of sulfur.

Mercaptans: Has smell often described as "garlic" or "skunky."

The following four terms describe off-odors resulting from the action of lactic acid on the developing wine.

Mousey: A sharp, pungent smell, brought on by the action of certain undesirable lactobacilli.[†]

[†]*Editor's Note:* Mousy/mousey off-flavor is an undesired and disagreeable flavor in wine that is redolent of mice (and the smells related to them). It is not perceived by sniffing the wine; rather it is perceived after the wine is swallowed or expectorated. It is caused by lactic acid bacteria produced by yeasts. It is not a volatile compound and therefore not detected by smell. Some individuals may be very sensitive and others may not be able to detect it at all.

Butrytic: Similar to the smell of rancid butter.

Acetic: The wine vinegar odor.

Lactic: Sometimes described as a "sauerkraut" smell.

The four terms listed below describe off-odors resulting from causes other than those mentioned in the previous sections.

Moldy: A readily recognized fault. A smell suggestive of moldy fruit or wood.

Raisiny: A smell reminding one of raisins or overripe grapes.

Woody: Suggestive of the odor of wet wood. (A trace of this smell, particularly that of oak, is desirable in a fine red table wine. It is an off-odor only when it is blatantly there.)

Corky: A smell resembling that of a dampened or moldy cork.

TASTE

True taste sensations are limited to sourness (acidity), sweetness, bitterness and saltiness. However, a trained palate can also measure viscosity (body) in a liquid, and can superimpose on its four basic tasting capacities certain judgments concerning a wine's flavor and age. The grouped terms below reflect this wide judging capacity.

Acidity

Flat: Possessing so little acid as to be hardly discernible.

Tart: Having a pleasant amount of acid; lively on the tongue but not excessively so.

Acidy: Having excessive acid content. Very sharp on the tongue.

Sweetness

Sweetness comes from the presence of sugars (glucose and fructose) in the wine, with glycerol contributing to the sweet taste. Acidity and astringency interact with the sweet impression, modifying it.

Dry: Possessing no discernible sweetness.

Low Sugar: Barely detectable sweetness.

Medium Sugar: Sweetness definitely there but subdued.

High Sugar: Unquestionably sweet.

Body

While body is not a "taste," it can be measured only by the mouth. Essentially, body is the "feel" of the wine as it is swished about in the mouth. It is almost impossible to describe. Recognition of "body" comes only from experience.

Light-or Thin-Bodied: Lacking a sense of viscosity; watery.

Medium-Bodied: Possessing discernible viscosity in the mouth.

Heavy-Bodied: Having a greater feel of viscosity.

Bitterness and Astringency

Though modified by other factors, particularly sugar, a wine tastes smooth, rough, puckery or bitter in good part because of the amounts and kinds of tannins it possesses. With age, astringency generally decreases but bitterness rarely disappears. A wine whose taste reminds you of caffeine or quinine[†] is not, nor is it likely to become, a good wine and should preferably be described as "bitter"—a term, incidentally, which does not appear in the Wine Institute guide. In this area of taste evaluation, the guide offers two pairs of descriptive terms.

Smooth; Soft: Without irritating astringency.

Slightly Rough; Very Rough: Describing increasing degrees of astringency.

Flavor

Describing the flavor of a wine generally means trying to relate it to a grape variety. However, alcohol is also considered as part of the wine's flavor, though it is generally not mentioned in describing a table wine unless it is found to be on the low or very high side. Evaluating a wine for flavor is therefore to all practical purposes measuring its relationship to a specific grape, as the term below reflects.

[†]*Editor's Note:* In terms of taste, quinine is a bitter-tasting flavor component as in tonic water.

Varietal: Possessing an ability to bring to mind the taste of a particular grape, thus clarifying or confirming a previously-made nasal determination.

Age

The age of a wine may be approximated by careful tasting, though proper age for a particular wine depends both on whether it is red or white (generally, the whites "age" more quickly than the reds) and on the variety or varieties of grapes used in its production.

Young: Fresh; generally low in bottle bouquet; sprightly; fruity.

Mature: Of sufficient age to have "wedded" its various components into a whole.

Aged: Possessing a mellowing balance due to proper period of cask and bottle maturation. Especially important in red wines.

Taste-Odors

The following terms, many of which would obviously be equally at home in the section describing odors, are listed under "taste" because they are best detected in the tasting evaluation.

Fruity: Possessing freshness, tartness and giving a fruit-like impression that is recognizable by both palate and nose.

Stemmy: Having a suggestion of bitterness as the result of being fermented in the presence of grape stems.

Gassy: Possessing a slight amount of dissolved carbon dioxide gas which nips the tongue; said of a still wine and not of an effervescent one.[†]

Metallic: Giving the palate an impression like that of tasing a piece of zinc or copper.

[†]*Editor's Note:* Carbon dioxide (a natural by-product of fermentation) gives wines "gassy" or "effervescent" qualities. Examples of still (non-sparkling) wines that are effervescent include some German Rieslings, Grüner Veltliner and Albariño. Effervescence in still wines can be caused if the wine is bottled before the residual sugars have been fully fermented or when bottling wine in cold temperatures, there may be more of the dissolved carbon dioxide still left in the wine after it is bottled.

Spoiled: Having a less-than-good taste as the result of spoilage or oxidation—or because the wine is so old that it has "gone to pieces."

Fresh: Possessing fruitiness and desirable tartness.

Clean: Proving free of both bacterial and processing defects.

Tired: Lacks freshness, fruitiness and aroma, suggesting that the wine has been excessively processed.

Well Balanced: Having its component substances in such relation to one another that the total impression is pleasant.

Unbalanced: Possessing an excessive amount of one or another flavor component to the point where the palate impression is that of taste disharmony.

Coarse; Harsh: Possessing an odor and/or taste in which acidity or astringency is excessive.

Foxy: Having the aroma and taste of Concord or other Labrusca grapes.

A final note: a yet unmentioned manner of describing a wine is one I have on occasion heard professional tasters use. It begins with the phrase, "This wine reminds me of . . ." and goes on from there to name a specific wine by brand and even year.

The meaningful use of the above phrase calls for what I consider exceptional taste memory. There are, in my judgment, comparatively few people who can correctly recall their sensory reactions to a particular wine tasted in other than the immediate past. If you happen to be such an individual,* my congratulations. You are legitimately entitled to tell your listeners that the wine under question seems to you to be quite similar to a named wine you had previously tasted.

Describing a wine in this manner, however, won't add much to the listener's understanding of the wine's quality unless he

---

*It seems to me that you can get at least an inkling of your taste memory by tasting (and drinking) a particular wine one evening and then, a week or ten days later, by having someone serve you blind a companion of this wine along with four or five similar wines. If you can, in three such tests, each time pick out the wine you first tasted, you, in my unscientific opinion, have it made as a taster.

too had previously tasted the referred-to wine and unless he too can recall the taste sensations it gave him. The "This reminds me of . . ." pattern therefore should be used only as a plus, as a supplement to the more particularized description provided through use of the terms listed above.[†]

◆ ◆ ◆

[†]*Editor's Note:* Another way to describe tasting components in wine: Body, Acidity, Texture, Aroma, Flavor, and Finish.

APPENDIX A

Recommended Aging for Wines

Note: The majority of table wines are usually meant to be consumed within a year or so. However, high-quality wines—made during the **best vintages** AND by the **best wine producers**—can be aged. The following are guidelines for aging wines.

White Wines

Non-Vintage Champagne	2 to 3+ years
French White Burgundy	2 to 10+ years
Chardonnay (California)	3 to 8+ years
German & Alsatian Riesling	3 to 30+ years
Gewürztraminer	3 to 30+ years
French Sauterne	3 to 30+ years
White Bordeaux	5 to 10+ years
Vintage Champagne (blanc-de-blancs)	10 to 15+ years

Red Wines

Pinot Noir (Oregon, California)	2 to 5+ years
Merlot (California)	2 to 10+ years
Red Burgundy (France)	3 to 8+ years
Chianti Classico (Riservas)	3 to 10+ years
Cabernet Sauvignon (California)	3 to 15+ years
Malbec (Argentina)	3 to 15+ years
Brunello di Montalcino	3 to 15+ years
Zinfandel (California)	5 to 15+ years
Rioja (Spain - Gran Reservas)	5 to 20+ years
Barolo & Barbaresco	5 to 25+ years
Syrah (Hermitage); Shiraz	5 to 25+ years
Bordeaux Chateaux	5 to 30+ years
Châteauneuf-du-Pape	7 to 10+ years
Port (vintage)	10 to 40+ years

◆ ◆ ◆

APPENDIX B

Suggested Wines for Comparison

(Same general type but with distinctive differences)

The following are some examples of a few wines that are the same type but have distinctive differences and may be a good way to determine taste similarities/dissimilarities.

Compare this wine . . .	*With this wine . . .*
Sauvignon Blanc	New Zealand Sauvignon Blanc
Beaujolais Nouveau	Other types of Beaujolais (non Nouveau)
California Chardonnay	White Burgundy (France)
Pinot Noir (Oregon/California)	French Burgundy
Australian Shiraz	French Syrah or California Syrah

◆ ◆ ◆

APPENDIX C

Describing Aromas & Flavors

The Wine Aroma Wheel was developed by Ann C. Noble, a sensory chemist and a former professor from the University of California, Davis. During her time there, she invented the aroma wheel to improve people's overall understanding of wine tasting and the terminology that applies to it. The categories are broken down into several groups, most with sub groups, that define the basic language used to categorize taste and aromas encountered in wine.

The categories and sub groups are:

Floral
– *orange blossom*
– *violet, rosé*
– *jasmine*
– *geranium*
– *linalool* (Earl Grey Tea)
– *terpene*

Earthy
– *moldy* (moldy *cooperage, moldy cork, must*)
– *earthy* (mushroom, dust)

Woody
– *burned* (coffee, burnt toast, smoky)
– *phenolic* (bacon, medicinal)
– *resinous* (vanilla, oak, cedar, pine, tobacco)

Spicy
– *anise*
– *licorice*
– *black pepper*
– *cloves*

Fruity
– *citrus* (grapefruit, lemon, orange)
– *berry* (blackberry, raspberry, strawberry, blackcurrant)
– *tree fruit* (cherry, apricot, peach, pear, apple)
– *tropical fruit* (pineapple, melon, banana)
– *dried fruit* (strawberry jam, raisin, prune, fig)
– *other* (methyl anthranilate/foxy, artificial fruit)

Vegetative/Herbaceous
– *fresh* (cut grass, green bell pepper, eucalyptus, mint)
– *dried* (hay, straw, tea)
– *canned/cooked* (green bean, asparagus, green olive, black olive, artichoke)

Chemical
– *petroleum* (tar, plastic, kerosene, diesel)
– *sulfur* (rubber, hydrogen sulfide, natural gas/mercaptan, garlic, skunk, cabbage, burnt match, wet wool, wet dog)
– *pungent* (ethyl acetate/nail polish remover, acetic acid/vinegar, ethanol, sulfur dioxide)

Caramel
– honey
– butterscotch
– butter
– soy sauce
– chocolate
– molasses

Oxidized—*sherry*

Micro Biological
– *yeasty* (baker's yeast, leesy)
– *lactic* (sauerkraut, sweaty, yogurt)
– *other* (horsey, mousey)

While the aroma wheel is not an exhaustive list of all wine aroma terms and categories that can be used, it provides a good foundation. These categories of aromas are helpful to understand not only as you recognize them while reading about a wine but also when evaluating and describing a wine yourself.

◆ ◆ ◆

APPENDIX D

Wine Rating Systems

Wine Spectator's 100–point scale

95–100 Classic: a great wine

90–94 Outstanding: a wine of superior character and style

85–89 Very good: a wine with special qualities

80–84 Good: a solid, well-made wine

75–79 Mediocre: a drinkable wine that may have minor flaws

50–74 Not recommended

Robert Parker's 100–point scale

96–100: An extraordinary wine of profound and complex character displaying all the attributes expected of a classic wine of its variety. Wines of this caliber are worth a special effort to find, purchase, and consume.

90–95: An outstanding wine of exceptional complexity and character. In short, these are terrific wines.

80–89: A barely above average to very good wine displaying various degrees of finesse and flavor as well as character with no noticeable flaws.

70–79: An average wine with little distinction except that it is a soundly made. In essence, a straightforward, innocuous wine.

60–69: A below average wine containing noticeable deficiencies, such as excessive acidity and/or tannin, an absence of flavor, or possibly dirty aromas or flavors.

50–59: A wine deemed to be unacceptable.

Wine Enthusiast

95–100—Superb. One of the greats.

90–94—Excellent. Extremely well made and highly recommended.

85–89—Very good. May offer outstanding value if the price is right.

80–84—Good. Solid wine, suitable for everyday consumption.

JamesSuckling.com

Run by the former European editor for Wine Spectator magazine, James Suckling will feature wine ratings and reviews for wines he rates with 90 points or higher.

Stephen Tanzer's International Wine Cellar

95–100—Extraordinary

90–94—Outstanding

85–89—Very Good to Excellent

80–84—Good

75–79—Average

70–74—Below Average

<70—Avoid

Wine & Spirits

80 to 85—good examples of their variety or region

86 to 89—highly recommended

90 to 94—exceptional examples of their type

95 to 100—superlative, rare finds

The majority of other notable wine publications providing wine ratings and scores use a 100-point scale largely similar to those listed above.

◆ ◆ ◆

APPENDIX E

Grape Varietals & Regional Wine Styles

The prominence of some wines and grape varieties referenced by the author in this book may have also changed over the years, so I have included a reference list of descriptions for readers to become better acquainted (or re-acquainted) with grape varieties and regional wines.

Grape Varietals:

Alicanté Bouschet A dark-skinned grape used more today for making port-style wines (a major grape grown in Portugal) or blended to add tannin or color to wines due to the grape's very dark and inky color.

Aligoté In Burgundy, France, this grape is used to make a dry white wine, but it can also be found in Russia, Bulgaria, Ukraine, Romania and Moldova. This variety can tolerate the cold and ripens early, producing wines with high acidity and the aroma of apples and lemons.

Almission A black grape that is a hybrid of the Mission grape and Carignan and is not prevalent as a varietal wine.

Barbera This grape is grown extensively in Italy and produced best in Piedmont and is known for its deep color and produces dark, fruity and sharp red wines, with flavors of blackberry and black cherry. Popular in California and Australia, it is also gaining ground in Argentina.

Cabernet Sauvignon One of the most well-known red wines, it is spicy and tannic with an undertone of black currant aroma. An original grape of the Médoc, it is also a popular grape variety grown in California, South America, Eastern Europe and even competes with popular Shiraz in Australia. This wine often benefits from being blended with Merlot, Cabernet Franc, Syrah and other red grapes and its best results are shown after the wine has aged.

Chardonnay A green-skinned non aromatic grape grown in several regions in France and around the world. Used for producing white wines, as well as Champagne and sparkling wines, with flavors and styles varying widely based on the amount of oak used in fermentation.

Chenin Blanc This high-acidity and high-sugar grape is used to produce a variety of still, sparkling and dessert-style wines. In cooler areas, the juice is sweet, but in warmer climates, the grapes are prone to sunburn due to tis thin skin, as well as bunch rot and over production.

Emerald Riesling A white hybrid-grape developed by a UC Davis professor in California ("Olmo grapes" named after the professor who created the varieties) is a cross between a Muscadelle and Riesling. It grows well in warm climates including South Africa. Produces medium-bodied wines that are highly acidic with floral aromas and a delicate fruity finish. While typically used to add acidity to bulk wines in California, Emerald Riesling is also produced as a single varietal wine in Israel.

Folle Blanche This grape is very good for producing brandy, because of the high acidity and low flavors, and is also used as table wine in the area of Loire Valley known as Gros Plant.

French Colombard This grape variety was grown traditionally for distilling into Cognac and Armagnac. It is now grown in the warmest areas of California and South Africa and produces a sharp, highly acidic and slightly fruity white wine.

Gamay This grape is an ancient clone of Pinot Noir and has bubble-gum, pear-like aromas. Best when young, the Gamay grape produces a light and fragrant wine is produced in Beaujolais France. Lighter wines are made from this grape in central France, Savoie and Switzerland. In California, it is also produced as Napa Gamay.

Gewürztraminer Also known as Traminer,this grape variety prefers cooler climates. With aroma similar to lychees, these grapes have a pink to red skin, which is high in natural sugar.

Grand Noir This hybrid red wine grape goes by other names in other countries (Spain Gran Nero; Portugal Baga) and is grown in Spain and in smaller amountsin France. The grape is used for blending red wines more for its heavy pigment rather than its flavor.

Green Hungarian A white-wine grape that produces pleasant, neutral wines having a slight "green" hue. Grown in limited amounts in California, these grapes produce wines with slightly sweet fruity flavors and bright acidity.

Grenache This grape is grown in southern France, Rioja Spain, California and South Africa. Wines produced from Grenache produce a pale, though rich and fruity wine used for port and rosé style wines. Some Grenache has higher alcohol content requiring the wine to be blended with other varieties. Old-vine Grenache is prized in South Australia. Also known as Cannonau in Italy and Garnacha in Spain.

Grignolino One of Piedmont's everyday table wines, these grapes produce light-colored red wines with strong tannins and acidity, and aromas that are fruity.

Malbec This is a major wine in Argentina but has been growing for years in south-western France (where it is known as Cot). The grapes produce a very dark and dense wine and have long been one of the six varieties permitted in the Bordeaux blend.

Merlot Though grassy when not completely ripe, this is a grape that adapts itself well to many areas. It has strong fruit flavors but has a very soft, velvety texture. The Merlot grape is a staple in Bordeaux wines.

Muscat Rarely used in dry wines, this grape is grown for raisins, table grapes and sweet and fortified wines. The grape's color can range from white to near black. Grown in many countries, it is one of the oldest domestic grape varieties.

Muscat of Alexandria Part of the Muscat family of grape varieties (known for producing pungent aromatics and sweet grape flavors), this particular grape is used primarily to produce sherry, muscatel wine and liqueurs. Also used for raisin production.

Nebbiolo This grape produces Barolo and Barbaresco; well-respected wines in Italy. Wine produced from the Nebbiolo grape is often softened with other grapes including Bonarda or Merlot.

This grape produces a fruity and intensely perfumed wine that improves with age.

Petite Sirah This is a cross of the Syrah and Peloursin grape. The grape produces dark colored and acidic wines with herbal, pepper and blueberry aromas and flavors. This wine has a long aging life and is deeper and fuller, yet brighter than Syrah.

Pinot Blanc This grape variety is good for producing young wines, and used in Italian Spumante. Wines usually show good balance between fruit flavors, nice acidity and alcohol.

Pinot Noir Famous in Burgundy for its smooth texture and subtle tannins along with a wine variety of flavors from berries to stone fruits. Grapes are used to produce single varietal still wines as well as sparkling wines. This wine is highly popular and is grown not only in France but throughout California, Oregon and New Zealand.

Port A sweet wine that is fortified with alcohol, named after the Douro Valley region in Portugal.

Red Veltliner/Roter Veltliner This is an Austrian red grape variety (roter means 'red') used to produce white wine that typically carries delicate spice aromas and rich honeyed raisin flavors balanced with lively acidity. A parent variety to many different Austrian Veltliner grapes, it is not related to Grüner Veltliner.

Refosco Also known as Mondeuse, this grape variety comes from Friuli, Italy and produces deep and full flavored wines when grown in warmer climates. The wines improve with age and are typically used for port-style wines.

Riesling This German grape produces white wines with very pronounced citrus and complex spice with minerality. As the wine ages, aromas are likened to the smell of gasoline which is seen as a positive. This grape is territorially ex¬pressive and the best wines of this varietal are from Alsace and Austria, where the wines are dry. Austrian Rieslings tend to lean more towards more tart and bright citrus lime-like flavors.

Rubired One of the "Olmo" grape varieties created by a UC Davis professor in California, this grape is a hybrid of the Alicanté

Bouschet grape and a Tinto Cao hybrid which gives wine produced by this grape a tinted (not clear) juice. Therefore, it is used to add dark color to red wines and developed to produce wines in the port style. Producers in Australia blend this in their fortified port wines.

Ruby Cabernet Another "Olmo" grape developed by UC Davis professor in California, this grape is a cross between Cabernet Sauvignon and Carignan grapes. Typically, used to add color and tannin to bulk wines, some producers have created varietal wines. Considered to produce wines that lack definition and body, wine produced by this grape is reminiscent of an under developed Cabernet Sauvignon and has the deep, dark color of the Carignan grape. Also grows well in hotter climates including South Africa, Australia, Argentina and Chile.

Salvador A hybrid grape grown in California for the purpose of adding deep dark colors to red wines.

Sauterne From the Bordeaux region of France, Sauterne is one of the most well-known dessert wines. With names such as Chateau d'Yquem, these wines have apricot, pineapple, or peach aromas with a creamy bruléed flavors.

Sauvignon Blanc These green-skinned grapes originate from France, and their flavor varies depending on the climate they are grown. Most notable areas are the Loire Valley, New Zealand and South Africa. Flavors for this white wine range from tart and grassy to sweet and tropical.

Sémillon Another green-skinned grape from Bordeaux that creates a sweet wine and is often blended with a Sauvignon Blanc.

Sylvaner This grape is primarily grown in Alsace and Germany with roots in Austria (known as Zierfandler). If the grapes are not controlled during the growth season, the wines can be somewhat bland. However, skilled winemakers will produce fine and elegant, fruity wines with high acidity.

Syrah/Shiraz(Known as Shiraz in Australia) This is a purple, peppery Rhône red grape that matures wonderfully. Goes by either name in California, Wash¬ington, Chile, South Africa and other areas.

Zinfandel This grape has long roots in history and is a popular variety grown in California. Wines can be produced as a red or rosé with blackberry flavors and a tannin structure that can sometimes be metallic.

Regional Wine Styles:

Barbaresco A full-bodied wine produced in the Piedmont region of Italy, with its high tannins and acidity, it is meant to be aged for several years to mellow. Like Barolo, this is an intensely-perfumed wine made from the same grape varietal, but is slightly less tannic and not as rich. See grape varietal *Nebbiolo*.

Barolo A rich, full-bodied wine produced in the Piedmont region of Italy, with its high tannins and acidity, it is meant to be aged for several years to mellow. An intensely-perfumed wine of black cherry, licorice, and even truffles with thick texture and a generous finish. See grape varietal *Nebbiolo*.

Bordeaux Blend The mixing together of several grape varietals (known to be grown in the Bordeaux region of France) to make a more complex red or white wine. Includes the following grapes for red: Cabernet Sauvignon, Merlot, Cabernet Franc, Petite Verdot, and Malbec; and for whites includes: Sauvignon Blanc and Sémillon.

Brunello di Montalcino Made from Sangiovese grapes, this wine comes from the town of Montalcino in the Tuscany region of Italy. It has fruity flavors comparable to strawberries. If the grapes are not tended to carefully, they are quite susceptible to rot.

Burgundy Refers to wines named after this region in France where they are produced. Red Burgundy is based on the Pinot Noir grape and White Burgundy is based on the Chardonnay grape. Red Burgundy generally differs from Pinot Noir produced in other countries in that Burgundy has less ripe-berry and more soil-like aromas, and can be aged longer than New World Pinot Noir. White Burgundy also has less fruity characteristics and more earthy aromas without the intense oak and buttery flavors as in California Chardonnay. French Burgundy wines are not overstated and are rather restrained in flavor and aroma as compared to their varietal counterparts in other countries.

Chablis These wines are also named after the Chablis area which is in the Burgundy region of France. While the term "Chablis" has been used to generally refer to ordinary bulk wines from other countries (due to the French not protecting the name), the true French Chablis is a high-quality and respected dry white wine with green-apple acidity, a flinty bouquet and mineral qualities that mellow to more subdued honey flavors when aged.

Châteauneuf-du-Pape This is the most famous wine region in Southern Rhone area of France and their wines (also by the same name) are based on blends of many types of grapes grown in the area usually with Grenache, Syrah, Mourvèdre (and more). The character of this wine is usually full-bodied with robust aromatics (ripe berries, toasted aromas, pepper, herbs and freshly earthed soil) and a long, lush finish.

Chianti A district in Italy's Tuscany region, Chianti is based on the Sangiovese grape. Paired well with high-acidity foods (e.g., tomato-based Italian dishes), this medium-bodied and moderate tannin wine is savory and spicy with more tart cherry and sour berry flavors. Chianti Classico also refers to a particular region that produces higher-quality Chianti and the Chianti Classico Riservas means that the wine has been aged before being released for sale.

Moselle/Mosel Refers to the wine produced in three countries along the Moselle (or Mosel) river: France, Luxembourg and Germany. Moselle wines are mainly white, made in some of the coldest climates producing wines with intense fruity aromatics and high acidity. Most known for Riesling, Müller Thurgau and Eiswein.

Rioja A major wine-producing region in Spain consisting of three areas: Rioja Alta, Rioja Alavesa, Rioja Baja. Most Rioja wines are red blends made primarily from Tempranillo and Garnacha (with some Graciano and Mazuelo). Rioja white wines are typically blends of Viura and Malvasia grapes. However, they also grow other grapes for varietal wines including Cabernet Sauvignon, Merlot and Chardonnay. Spanish red wines that carry the 'Gran Reserva' designation indicate that the wine is at least five years old and has been aged for 18 months in oak.

Sauternes A dessert wine produced from late-harvested overripe Sémillon and Sauvignon Blanc grapes from France's Bordeaux region, producing sweet, honeyed, fruity and luscious wines balanced with acidity. Served mostly with moderately sweet desserts or fruit but can be tried with salty, rich fatty foods (e.g. foie gras).

◆ ◆ ◆

GLOSSARY

Acescence The presence of acetic acid which can lead to wine becoming vinegar and/or producing a vinegary off-aroma.

Acetic acid One of the critical volatile acids present in all wines that, in the right amount, enhances the flavor. Excess amounts of acetic acid produce a vinegar taste in wine.

Acidity Refers to the level of tartness in a wine based on the acids present in the grape. These acids help counteract the sugar and balances out the flavor of the wine.

Aftertaste (referred to as 'finish' in wine tasting) The flavor that lingers in the mouth after the wine has been swirled around and expectorated or swallowed. The aftertaste can be long or short, with a longer time being preferable.

Aerate Occurs when wine is opened and meets the air (either in the bottle or by being poured into a glass). The air helps release the flavor of the wine.

Alcohol In wine, this refers to ethyl alcohol, which acts like a preservative in wine, thus allowing it to age. It is a by-product of fermentation.

Appearance Refers to how a wine looks, usually defined by its color, clarity, and brightness.

Aroma Used to refer to the smells of the wine, typically the fruity or fresh smells (such as currant, apple, and pear). The longer a wine ages, the less fruit-based aroma it will have. (See also *bouquet*).

Astringency Sharp or pungent acidic tones or flavors.

Balance Used to describe wine that has symmetry in all of the wine's elements including alcohol, acidity, tannin, and flavor.

Bitterness Often related to sharper tannins in a wine which may be reduced or mellowed with aging.

Blanc de Blancs (French) Term usually used for sparkling wines, this translates to "white of whites" referring to a white wine made from white grapes.

Blend Combining wines from different grape varieties, regions, barrel aging methods or vintages to create a wine of better quality. Blending occurs after the wines have been fermented.

Blind tasting A wine tasting where the information about the wine is withheld until participants have first assessed and evaluated the wines.

Body The perceived lightness or heaviness of a wine in the mouth.

Bottle Aging After a wine has been fermented and bottled, it is allowed to age in the bottle for a period of time until it is consumed. Bottle aging allows the wine to mature and become smoother.

Bouquet (French) Term used to describe the combination of aromas detected in the wine, usually referring to those associated with the maturing process (e.g., vanilla, oak, honey).

Brilliant Refers to the appearance of a wine where clarity seems free of all suspended material.

Brut (French) Typically used to refer to sparkling wines, this term describes very dry wines with little residual sugar.

Claret An English term for a red Bordeaux wine.

Clarity/Clear A clear wine or a wine with good clarity has no particles or other floating substances to interfere with its appearance when observed in the glass.

Closed A wine-tasting term used to describe when a wine's aroma or flavor qualities are "hidden" or hard to detect due to the wine's youth. These qualities may open up with additional aging time in the bottle.

Cloudiness A wine that is cloudy has particles present in the wine that can affect the taste by making it seem murky; usually the mark of a bad or spoiled wine.

Cloying A wine quality used to describe a wine that may be initially pleasant but causes distaste due to excess sweetness.

Color The color of wine is an indicator of the age of the wine and can give some cues as to the quality. Red wines range in color from purple, ruby, red and brown hues. White wines range in color from pale yellow-green, straw, gold and brown hues. Rosés range in color from pink to orange. As white wines age, they gain color. Red wines lose color as they age.

Complexity Refers to the collective variety of different flavors and aromas of a wine that affect the taste as well as the aftertaste.

Corked Refers to a defective wine with undesirable smells or tastes (usually like a moldy attic or cardboard box) that are detected after bottling, aging and opening.

Crisp A wine-tasting term used to describe wine that has prominent acidity and a clean or refreshing finish.

Dry/Dryness A wine that is low in sugar, having been converted to alcohol, and therefore is not sweet; can also indicate a high level of acidity.

Dull Refers to the appearance of a wine where clarity is lacking and haziness is readily noticeable yet not quite cloudy.

Dump Bucket Casual term for the container offered during wine tastings to dump out any excess wines from the tasting glass or for spitting.

Earthy A wine-tasting term used to define aromas likened to earthy materials (e.g., mushrooms or freshly turned soil). Too much earthiness may actually cause the wine to taste corked.

Effervescence Carbon dioxide (a natural by-product of fermentation) gives wines "gassy" or "effervescent" qualities. Effervescence in still wines can give off tiny bubbles and are caused if the wine is bottled before the residual sugars have been fully fermented or if some of the dissolved carbon dioxide is still left in the wine after it is bottled (especially when bottling wine in cold temperatures).

Esters Sweet-smelling aromatic compounds, formed during fermentation and throughout a wine's maturation. Esters contribute to a wine's aroma and bouquet.

Expectorate A nice way of saying "to spit out."

Fermentation The chemical process by which yeasts interact with sugars to create alcohol and carbon dioxide, thus making wine from the juice of grapes.

Filtering Removing unwanted particles in the wine such as suspended solids, yeast or malolactic bacteria. This can be done through different methods such as passing the wine through membranes, cellulose pads or diatomaceous earth. Sweet wines must be filtered to remove yeast and prevent re-fermentation in the bottle. Too much filtration can strip a wine's flavor and aroma.

Finish A wine tasting term used to describe the final impression that a wine leaves in the mouth after the taste is gone, demonstrating the longevity of the wine's characteristics in the mouth.

Firm A wine tasting term used to describe a wine with substantial tannins or acidity.

Flabby A wine tasting term used to describe when a wine is dull or lacks acidity.

Flat Refers to a still wine that is lacking acidity and thus tastes dull (or a sparkling wine that has lost its bubbles).

Flavor The sensory impression that a food or wine gives as determined by the senses of taste and smell.

Flight A selection of wines for tasting (usually between 3-8 glasses).

Foxy Used to describe a wine that has aromas and tastes of very sweet and cloying "grapey" qualities much like Concord grape juice.

Fruity A wine that has an aroma relating to a fruit, such as pear, apple, cherry, black currant, and raspberry. Mostly present in young wines without much aging.

Gasoline In wine tasting, this is an aroma element that finer, mature Rieslings can demonstrate along with honey, citrus and zesty notes. This gasoline-like character is not necessarily a negative aspect of the wine and such Rieslings can be paired well with rich, buttery, earthy foods (e.g., foie gras).

Grassy A wine tasting term used to describe white wines that have aromas or flavors of cut grass or greens and is usually refreshing.

Herbaceous A wine tasting term indicating aromas and flavors of herb or vegetative characters (i.e. bell pepper, black olive, asparagus, tomato leaf).

Horizontal Tasting A selection of wines for tasting that are all from the same vintage or follow the same wine-making style.

Hotness A term used to describe the effects of the component of alcohol in wine. The amount of alcohol contained in the wine will give tasters the perception of "heat" or hotness in the back of the mouth. High-alcohol wines are sometimes referred to as being "hot" and must be considered when pairing wine with spicy food.

Initial Taste The first impression of a wine when it hits the mouth.

Inky Refers to the appearance of red wine that is so dark, it is opaque.

Jammy Refers to red wine that is rich in fruit.

Lactic Acid Refers to the smoother lactic acid or milk taste developed in wine through malolactic fermentation.

Lactobacillus A microscopic bacteria that can cause damage to wines by producing excessive acetic acid, slowing or stopping the wine's fermentation, causing spoilage of the wine (if sulfur dioxide has not yet been added), and in some cases may cause the "mousy" off-flavor in wine.

Lees Dead yeast cells left behind after the fermentation process.

Legs The long marks left on the side of a wine glass consisting of wine droplets as a wine is swirled in the glass.

Malic Acid Refers to the harsh-tasting acid present typically present in apples. Malic acid in wine is changed into softer lactic acids through malolactic fermentation.

Malolactic Fermentation A type of fermentation where a chemical process converts malic acid into lactic acid giving wine a much smoother taste.

Maturation The process of aging wine in wood (such as an oak barrel) versus a bottle.

Mouthfeel The tactile sensations of wine in the mouth.

Non-Vintage (NV) Denotes a wine that is a blend of grapes from different years as well as different vineyards and varietals (e.g., as in Non-Vintage Champagne).

Nose Refers to the expression of a wine's aroma and bouquet.

Oaky A wine tasting term used to describe a wine that has aged too long in oak, causing the flavor of the oak to overpower the flavor of the grape.

Oenologist One who is engaged in wine making. Also called Enologist.

Off-dry Not quite dry; a perception of sweetness too faint to call the wine sweet.

Olfactory Nerve The nerve that perceives aromas, therefore engaging the sense of smell.

Orthonasal Refers to the aroma perceptions introduced to the olfactory nerve orthonasally through the nose versus the mouth.

Oxidized/Oxidation Refers to wine exposed to oxygen. While all wines are exposed to certain amounts of oxygen throughout the production and aging process, generally an "oxidized" wine means that it has been exposed to oxygen in such a way that it negatively changes the quality of the wine, causing the wine to lose some of its flavor and freshness.

Palate When used in conjunction with the subject of wine, palate refers to a person's particular taste interpretation, sense of taste and flavor.

PH Measurement of the acidity of a wine. The lower the PH, the higher the acidity.

Phenolic A group of chemical compounds known as polyphenols that have an effect on wine color, taste, and sensation. Phenols are introduced through tannins from the grape skins or through oak aging and can result in vanillin or even medicinal aromas and flavors.

Precipitate Part of the natural aging process of red wines, precipitate is the by-product of tannin compounds combining with natural pigments in the wine that "precipitates" (or separates) out as a fine suspension of solid particles. This results in a smoother and clearer wine. Precipitate is usually seen along the inside surface of the bottle and is not harmful. The wine can usually be poured without the particles getting into the glass (if the bottle hasn't been disturbed) although it is preferable to decant before pouring if precipitate is particularly heavy.

Primary Fermentation Refers to the first stage of fermentation in the vinification process where yeasts convert sugars in the grape juice to alcohol and carbon dioxide.

Pyrazine A compound that gives wine a bell-pepper flavor that decreases in strength as the grapes ripen.

Redolent A term often used to indicate that a wine is suggestive, reminiscent or has the smell of certain fragrant and aromatic or sweet scents.

Reserve An amount of wine set aside by the winemaker to be aged longer or produced to a superior quality and is typically offered in more limited production.

Residual Sugar The sugar content that is left in a wine after fermentation.

Reticent A term used to indicate when a wine's bouquet is restrained or holds back its aromas generally due to its youth.

Retronasal Refers to the aroma perceptions introduced to the olfactory nerve retronasally through the mouth with the air we breathe.

Secondary Fermentation The fermentation process in Méthode Champenoise which occurs in the bottle by adding a small amount of sugar and yeast. The yeast and sugar interact within the sealed bottle, creating alcohol and carbon dioxide. This gas in the bottle gives sparkling wine its effervescence.

Semi-blind A taster knows only the style of the wine (grape) or where it comes from.

Sensory Evaluation Relating to the using the senses of sight (appearance), touch (texture), smell (aroma) and taste (flavor) in wine tasting in order to assess a wine's characteristics, to describe what sensations the taster is experiencing and ultimately, evaluate whether the taster likes or dislikes a wine.

Stemmy/Stemminess A term for wines that exhibit harsh, bitter or astringent characteristics in a wine as a result of being fermented too long with the grape stems. This quality can be pleasant or unpleasant, depending upon how dominant the stemmy or "green" quality overshadows the actual fruit.

Structure Refers to a wine's mouth feel as related to the balance of alcohol with the wine's tannins, acidity, sugar and fruit flavor.

Sulfur dioxide Sulfur dioxide is used during the fermentation process to slow the process of the wine oxidizing thus giving the wine a longer shelf life.

Tannins A compound that is found naturally in grape skins seeds and stems, as well as oak barrels that causes a wine to taste more tart. Older reds that have aged longer have less tannin than younger ones and are therefore less sharp.

Tartrates Naturally-occurring deposits of tartaric acid emanating from the wine which may concentrate to look like crystals and appear on the bottom of the cork or may fall to the bottom of the bottle.

Tawny Used to describe a wine color that has orange-brown or yellowish-brown hues. Typically prevalent in older or aged wines and some dessert wines (e.g., Port, aged Sauterne, Madeira).

Terroir (French) Refers to the characteristics that wine derives from the location in which it was grown, including everything from climate, soil, native vegetation, slope angle, and air quality. Also refers to the notion of placing importance on the provenance or types of grapes produced by a certain terroir rather than on the vintner or winemaker.

Texture Refers to how the wine feels in the mouth (e.g. smooth and velvety or harsh and biting).

Ullage (French) The gap between the top of the wine bottle and the wine.

Unctuous Oily, greasy or fatty in taste.

Unfiltered Wines that have not gone through a filtering process to remove suspended materials that occur as part of the winemaking process. Some winemakers do not filter their wines as they believe filtering may diminish flavor.

Varietal The specific type of grape; also a wine that is named after the variety of grape used to produce the wine.

Vertical Tasting A selection of wines for tasting featuring the same type of wines made from different vintages.

Vinification The process of making wine from grapes.

Vinous Literally means "wine like" and is usually applied to dull wines lacking in distinct varietal character.

Vintage When on a bottle, it refers to the year the grapes were harvested.

Viscosity Refers to the consistency of fluid that causes it to resist flowing. Viscosity is used to indicate a wine's body and potential quality.

Volatile/Volatility Refers to a substance that changes readily from solid or liquid to a vapor. The level at which vaporization of a wine's aromas occurs (or volatility) dictates the perception of flavor perceived through aromas received through the nose (orthonasal) or the mouth (retronasal).

Weight Refers to the feel of wine on the palate and is closely associated with the body of the wine.

Woody Similar to the term oaky, it refers to wines that have aged for too long in an oak barrel and have taken on the flavor and aroma of the wood.

Yeast A single-celled fungi that is added to grapes to aid in converting the sugar to alcohol and releasing carbon dioxide, thus fermenting the wine.

◆ ◆ ◆

POSTSCRIPT

Whether you have gone through the entire series of tests offered in the preceding chapters or have, at the other extreme, merely skimmed through this little volume without actually undergoing any self testing, you should to a greater or lesser degree be better equipped than you previously were to evaluate wines on their merits rather than on their costs or their brands.

True, wine prices and wine brands are generally indicative of the quality classifications into which wines fall, but this is not always so. Occasionally a low priced wine develops into a beautifully rounded, near classical beverage; and occasionally a high priced wine, for one reason or another (often having nothing to do with the man who produced it) reaches your glass in poor condition.

As regards brand names, these can usually be counted on to provide you with that for which they have become known, be it for a line of good everyday wines, wines of medium quality or true classics of their kind. From time to time, however, a wine unexpectedly steps out of the class for which its brand is widely known, with this step leading either upward or downward.

The real measure of a wine, then—and I repeat myself deliberately here in order to emphasize this point—lies in the pleasure or lack of it the wine brings the imbiber. To make such a yardstick valid, however, it must be assumed that the imbiber possesses the capacity to recognize when a wine is poor, is fair, is good or is extraordinary. Hopefully this booklet has helped you achieve a higher-than-before level of such discrimination.

Enjoy.

Irving H. Marcus

Lightning Source UK Ltd.
Milton Keynes UK
UKHW02f1849290718
326464UK00012B/164/P